The Ponytail Girls

A Stormy Spring

LEGACY PRESS

Other books in the Ponytail Girls series:

Book 1
Meet the Ponytail Girls

Book 2
The Impossible Christmas Present

Book 3
Lost on Monster Mountain

Book 5
Escape from Camp Porcupine

The Ponytail Girls

A Stormy Spring

Bonnie Compton Hanson

Dedication

For my granddaughter, Phoebe,
and all the rest of you wonderful girls.

THE PONYTAIL GIRLS/BOOK 4: A STORMY SPRING

ISBN 1-58411-032-5
Legacy reorder# LP48044

Legacy Press
P.O. Box 261129
San Diego, CA 92196

Illustrator: Aline Heiser

Printed in the United States of America

Contents

Chapter 15

Chapter 16

Chapter 17

Chapter 18

Chapter 19

Extra Stuff!

~ Introduction ~

Welcome to the Ponytail Girls! Whether you wear a ponytail or not you can share in the adventures of Sam Pearson and her friends, the PTs (that's short for Ponytails!). Just like you, the PTs love sports and shopping and fun with their friends at school.

The PTs also want to live in a way that is pleasing to God. So when they have problems and conflicts, they look to God and His Word, the Bible. They might also seek help from their parents, their pastor or their Sunday school class teacher, just like you do.

Each chapter in this book presents a new problem for your PTs to solve. Then there is a Bible story to help explain the Christian value that the PTs learned. A Bible memory verse is included for you to practice and share.

There may be words in this book that are new to you, especially some Bible names and Spanish words. Look them up in the Glossary on page 187, then use the syllables to sound out the words.

In addition to the stories, in each chapter you will find questions to answer and fun quizzes, puzzles and other activities. Also, at the end of each chapter starting with Chapter 1, you will get a clue that leads to the finished Joyful Easter Puzzle at the end of the book. Don't forget to fill in the puzzle so you can see the secret message!

The fun doesn't end with the stories. At the end of the book, you'll find information and membership cards for starting your own Ponytail Girls Club. A list of the memory verses in the book is on page 185. The answers to the puzzles (not that you'll need them!) are on page 189.

The first Ponytail Girls book, *Meet the Ponytail Girls,* began just before school started in the fall. In *The Impossible Christmas Present,* you followed the PTs through the tragedies and triumphs of their holiday season. *Lost on Monster Mountain* saw the PTs off to Winter Camp with their Madison classmates. After you see what happens to the PTs during the spring, be sure to catch up with them again in the next book, *Escape from Camp Porcupine,* as they head off to summer camp.

Meet Your Ponytail Girls!

· WHO ARE THEY? ·

The Ponytail Girls are girls your age who enjoy school, church, shopping and being with their friends and family. They also love meeting new friends. Friends just like you! You will like being a part of their lives.

The PTs all attend Madison Middle School in the small town of Circleville. They're all also members of Miss Kotter's Sunday school class at nearby Faith Church on Sunday mornings. On Sunday evenings, they attend the special Zone 56 youth group for guys and girls their age. Their pastor is Reverand J. T. McConahan, and their youth leader is Pastor Andrew Garretti, whom they call "Pastor Andy."

Sam and Sara grew up in Circleville. Le's and LaToya's families moved into their neighborhood last year. When Sam and Sara met them at school, they invited them to church. Then Maria moved to Circleville and she became a PT, followed by Jenna and Sonya. Now it would be hard for all seven of them to imagine not being PTs!

How did the PTs get their club name? Well, as you can see from their pictures, they all wear a ponytail of one kind or another. So that's what their other friends and families started calling them just for fun. Then one day LaToya shortened it to "PTs." Now that's what they all call themselves!

The PTs' club meetings are held whenever they can all get together. The girls have a secret motto: PT4JC, which means "Ponytails for Jesus Christ." They also have a secret code for the club's name: a "P" and a "T" back to back. But most of the time they don't want to keep secrets. They want to share with everyone the Good News about their best friend, Jesus.

Have fun sharing in your PTs' adventures. Laugh with them in their silly time, think and pray with them through their problems. And learn with them that the answers to all problems can be found right in God's Word. Keep your Bible and a sharpened pencil handy. Sam and the others are waiting for you!

GET TO KNOW THE PTS

Sam Pearson *has a long blond ponytail, sparkling blue eyes and a dream: she wants to play professional basketball. She also likes to design clothes. Sam's name is really "Samantha," but her friends and family just call her "Sam" for short. Sam's little brother, Petie, is 7. Joe, her dad, is great at fixing things, like cars and bikes. Her mom, Jean, bakes scrumptious cakes and pies and works at the Paws and Pooches Animal Shelter. Sneezit is the family dog.*

LaToya Thomas' *black curls are ponytailed high above her ears. That way she doesn't miss a thing going on! LaToya's into gymnastics and playing the guitar. Her big sister, Tina, is in college, training to be a nurse. Her mom is a school teacher; her dad works nights at a supermarket. Also living with the Thomases is LaToya's beloved, wheelchair-bound grandmother, Granny B.*

Le Tran *parts her glossy black hair to one side, holding it back with one small ponytail. She loves sewing, soccer and playing the violin. Her mother, Viola, a concert pianist, often plays duets with her. Her father, Daniel, died in an accident. but he became a Christian before he died. Le's mother was a Buddhist but she recently became a new Christian.*

• Le Tran •

Sara Fields *lives down the street from Sam. She keeps her fiery, red hair from flying away by tying it into a ponytail flat against each side of her head. Sara has freckles, glasses and a great sense of humor. She loves to sing. She also loves softball, ice skating and cheerleading. Sara has a big brother, Tony, and a big dog, Tank. Both her parents are artists.*

• Sara Fields •

When **Maria Moreno** *moved in next door to Sam in September, she became the fifth PT. Maria pulls part of her long, brown hair into one topknot ponytail at the back; the rest hangs loose. She is tall, the way basketball-lover Sam would like to be! But Maria's into science, not basketball. At home, she helps her mother take care of her 6-year-old twin brothers, Juan and Ricardo, and a little sister, Lolita. The Morenos all speak Spanish as well as English.*

• Miss Kotter •

Miss Kitty Kotter, *the girls' Sunday school teacher, is not a PT, but she is an important part of their lives both in church and out of church. Miss Kotter is single and works as a computer engineer. She also loves to go on hikes. Miss Kotter calls the Bible her "how-to book" because, she says, it tells "how to" live. Miss Kotter volunteers at the Circleville Rescue Mission.*

Jenna Jenkins *is tall and wears her rich auburn ponytail high on her head, like a crown. Jenna loves ballet, her little sister Katie and the adorable new twins, Noel and Holly, who were born at Christmas time. Jenna's mom makes delicious cookies. Jenna's dad is an accountant.*

Sonya Silverhorse *is disabled and uses a wheelchair. She has a sweet smile. Her bouncy cocker spaniel's name is Cocky. Sonya wears her coal-black ponytail long and braided in honor of her Cherokee background. She and her dad are new in town. He is Mr. Moreno's and Mr. Pearson's new boss. Her mother died in the accident that disabled Sonya.*

Get ready for fun with the PTs!

Chapter 1

Go Fly a Kite

Brittany Boorsma had never been happier in her life. In January, her parents had split up. But now they were back together and going to marriage counseling every week. Even though they still had a lot of problems, they had stopped arguing all the time. In fact, her mom had started attending Faith Church with her every week.

Church — wow! Being a new Christian — wow! Brittany was excited about all of the changes in her life. Before she became a Christian, Brittany had been a snob. She said mean things to people and made fun of anyone who was not like her. When her parents almost divorced, Brittany attempted suicide.

Brittany's mother bought her a new Bible with her name printed in gold ink on the cover. So Brittany decided to start right at the front of the Bible and read the whole thing through. *Boy, God will be proud of me then*, she thought.

She also decided to never miss a church service, Sunday school class or Zone 56 meeting. *That would show God how thankful I am for all He has done for me*, she reasoned, *including sending those two stray dogs to save my life on Monster Mountain. And then working it out so I could keep them as pets!*

"Brittany," her mother said when they first brought her new dogs home, "You know I'm at work all day, so you'll have to take over the responsibility for Hope and Sweetie. That means giving them food and water every single day. Exercising them, too. And don't forget to take a pooper scooper when you are out of the yard. We don't want to leave any surprises for the neighbors."

"Oh, sure, Mom!" Brittany said. "No problem! That'll be fun!"

Well, remembering to get the dogs' food and water twice a day — every day — was hard enough. But walking them outside in the deep snow, especially when they wanted to run, not walk, (and run in two different directions!) got old fast.

Fortunately, Brittany, who had tried to commit suicide at her school's Winter Camp, no longer had to use crutches. But she still found it hard to walk with some of her toes amputated. She also found it very easy to feel sorry for herself, especially when she'd much rather be at the shopping mall talking with her friends than taking care of dogs.

After one especially grumpy day, Brittany really didn't want to open her Bible, but she did anyway. She was still reading Genesis and there was so much for her to think about! She'd never even considered how creation happened until she read about it. And then she found it hard to relate to Adam and Eve, the very first people. What would it have been like to be created as an adult and never have to go to school? Or get to go shopping?

On this particular day, Brittany was reading chapter 3 in Genesis. Up until then she had thought Eve was pretty cool, with a great life. After all, she only had to run around playing with animals all day. She never had to do homework or dishes!

But as she read more, Brittany got angry at Eve. Why in the world did she eat something she shouldn't eat? Why in the world did she lie? Sinning is so dumb, Brittany thought as she slammed her Bible closed. It just gets people into trouble. And then they have to tell God they are sorry and ask Him to help them.

"I am through with sinning," she said aloud to herself as she poured a glass of orange juice. "Yep! No more being selfish or losing my temper or yelling at anyone. Then I won't get into trouble the way Eve did."

Just then, her phone rang. It was Jenna Jenkins. "Hey, Brittany!" she said. "Saturday the PTs are all getting together at the Bark Park with our dogs and our little brothers and sisters, if the weather's good. We want to play Frisbee and fly kites. Want to bring your pooches and join us? That park's fenced off, you know, so the dogs can run free. We'll have a blast!"

Brittany thought a minute. Hope and Sweetie could be a real handful. But if they ran around and played with the other dogs, she wouldn't have to watch them all the time. And she did love to fly kites. Besides, she liked that Jenna considered her a PT, too.

"Sure, we'll come," Brittany decided.

That Saturday a great March wind practically blew everyone all the way to the dog park. They had to hold tight to their new kites to keep them from being yanked right out of their hands.

Once they reached the park, the PTs helped the younger kids attach strings and tails to their kites. Then they showed their brothers and sisters how to help the kites catch the wind. Soon Jenna's sister Katie; Sam Pearson's brother, Petie; and Maria Moreno's twin brothers, Ricardo and Juan, were handling their kites like pros.

Sam's cousin Suzie had come along, too. At first her kite kept nosediving, but finally she got the hang of it. The kites looked like bits of rainbows in the sky as they flew together in red, yellow, blue, green and orange.

Then the PTs launched their own kites. Even Sonya Silverhorse, who was disabled and in a wheelchair, soon had one soaring high above. Brittany's, though, was the grandest of all: a super-big dragon kite with a long, floppy tail. "Don't let the other kites get near mine!" she snapped. "Mine's the most expensive and best. I don't want it to get messed up."

The other girls gave her a surprised look. They liked the new Brittany they'd come to know recently. Was the old, mean Brittany coming back?

Brittany waved her kite back and forth to keep the other kites away. Then she ran the best she could with her bad foot straight up the hill. "I'm highest of all!" she shouted, as she headed for some trees.

"Woof!" cried Brittany's dogs as they ran after her, tails wagging rapidly. Then the other dogs ran after them! They all rushed right up to Brittany, jumping all over her and each other in their excitement.

Down went Brittany. Down went all the dogs on top of her and each other. And down came her grand dragon kite crashing right into a tree.

"Stupid dogs!" she screeched as the other kids came running to help.

Whining pitifully, the animals tried to lick and nuzzle her. Then when they realized she was mad at them, they hung their heads and stuck their tails between their legs in sorrow.

As she was brushing the grass and dirt off her clothes, Brittany suddenly remembered her promise to herself never to sin again. And here she was yelling and being selfish! She understood now how easy it was to be tempted and give in to bad things if she didn't ask God to help her do right.

Brittany reached down and gathered together as many dogs as she could. She gave each one a hug. "I'm sorry, guys," she said.

She also apologized to the PTs, and to God. *Please help me do better next time!* she prayed.

· Good News · from God's Word

This is the story Brittany read about the world's very first woman.

Eve's Repentance

FROM GENESIS 2:21-3:24

Did you ever hear about something being "just perfect"? We all use that term at times, but we don't really mean it. After all, if the dress you found on sale was really "just perfect," you'd never want another dress, would you? What we really mean by "just perfect" is that something is very, very nice. But long ago, a woman did indeed have everything perfect. Her name was Eve.

God had created a perfect world. Even the animals were all friends with each other. In this perfect world, He created a perfect Garden of Eden, large enough for people to move around in and explore, but small enough for them to take care of. It was full of all kinds of plants and animals.

Then God created the first man, Adam, and put him in this garden. Next, He created the first woman, Eve. They loved God, they loved each other, they loved their new home. Everything was perfect.

There was just one thing in this wonderful garden that God said not to do. Adam and Eve were not to eat from a special tree, called the Tree of Knowledge of Good and Evil.

One day Satan said to Eve, "God's being so selfish. He doesn't want you to be happy. If you go ahead and eat from the tree that teaches about good and evil, you'll be as important as God is! Besides, take my word for it: that tree's fruit is deeee-lish!"

So Eve took a look at the fruit. *What could be wrong with just looking?* she thought. Then she picked a piece of fruit from the tree. Was that wrong? No. But then she tasted it, and gave some to Adam for him to taste. Was that wrong? YES!

The tree did teach about good and evil. It taught that obeying God is good and disobeying Him is evil. But Satan lied, as he always does. Adam and Eve didn't become as important as God when they ate from that tree. And the fruit of disobeying wasn't delicious — it was terrible. It was sin!

Adam and Eve were very sorry for doing wrong. They were also sorry for their punishment, which meant they had to leave the Garden and work hard to live. They learned that people can't do right all the time on their own. When we do sin, we need to repent and ask God to forgive us, then to help us do better next time!

A Verse to Remember

Godly sorrow brings repentance.

— 2 Corinthians 7:10

Now Read This!

Yes, all of us sin and do wrong things — just like Brittany did. But here's what God wants us to do:

- Recognize what we did wrong.
- Realize that it not only hurts us when we sin, but it may hurt others also.
- Repent and tell God we're sorry.
- Request God to forgive us (He always will!) and help us do better.
- Renew our desire to resist temptation next time.

What About You?

What tempts you the most? What causes you the most problems, such as losing your temper, being crabby, watching too much TV, not studying and so on? Write your temptations here:

____

____

Write today's date here: _____________ .

Ask God to help you do better starting right now!

A Perfect Puzzle

The Joyful Easter Puzzle on the next page is about someone who is perfect: Jesus, and about a time of great joy: Easter. Each chapter of this book will give you a Secret Letter to add to one of the spaces in the puzzle. The first last letter is already filled in for you. When the puzzle is complete, copy the letters in order onto the spaces below the puzzle. You will discover a joyful Easter message! For today, add the Secret Letter "R" for "repentant" to space 7 of the puzzle.

___ ___ ___ ___ ___   ___ ___ ___ ___ ___!

___ ___ ___ ___ ___ ___ ___ ___ ___ ___ ___!

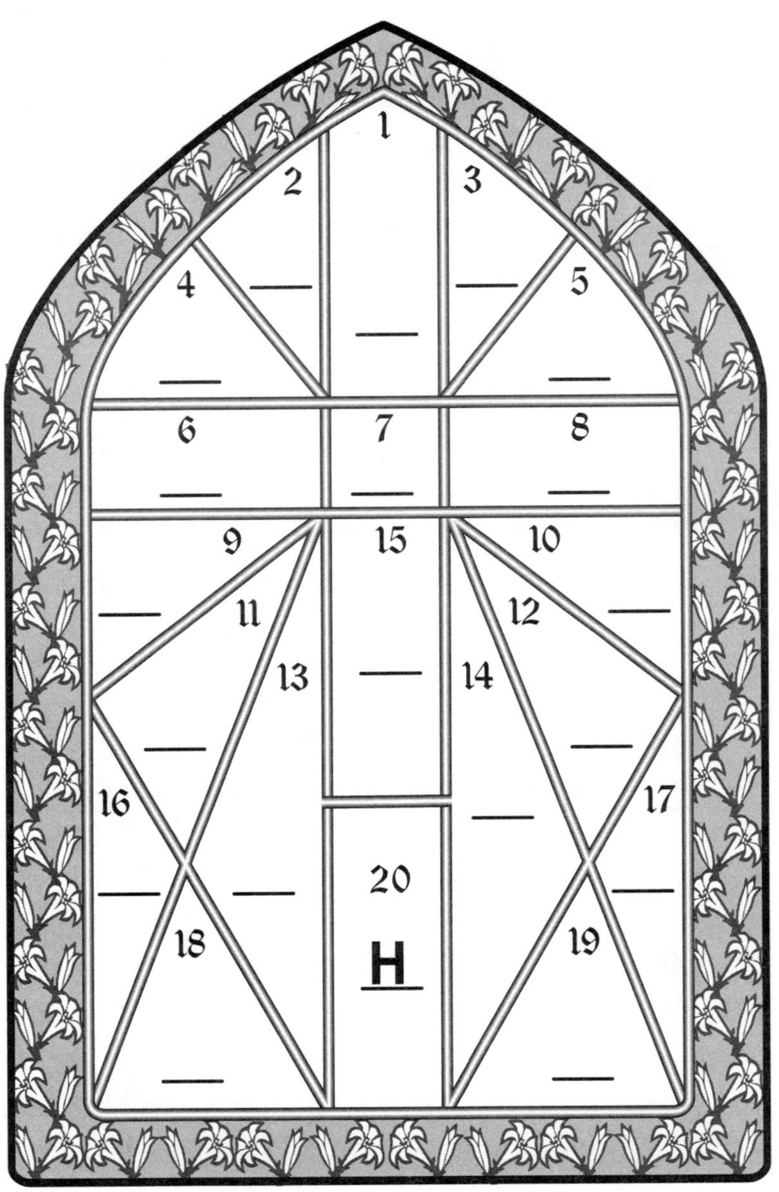
1
2
3
4
5
6
7
8
9
10
11
12
13
14
15
16
17
18
19
20
H

Chapter 2

It's Our Only Hope!

The calendar didn't say it was spring yet, but a blazing sun did. Fluffy, white clouds skipped across a bright blue sky.

The grass was still dead and brown. And the trees were as bare as ever. But Sam knew it was spring anyway. She could feel it in her bones. Besides, she just saw the very first crocus blooming.

"It must be spring fever!" she confided to Sara Fields, another PT. "I'm just dying to take a trip.

Somewhere far away and exotic."

Sara laughed. "Would Midland do? Mom and Dad have been invited to set up an exhibit at the Bon Jour Art Gallery there. So they're taking their paintings over tomorrow after school. Tony and I are going along to help. We're taking the van, so there should be plenty of room for you, too."

"That is," Sara added, grinning, "if you don't mind having a lap full of canvases."

Sam laughed. "Not at all, as long as the paint's dry. Maybe we can give Shannon a call and she could meet us there. Wouldn't that be great?"

Shannon Hendricks lived in Midland. She was a Christian, too. The PTs had met her at Winter Camp, where they all became friends. In fact, just a couple of weeks earlier their churches had held a praise band night together.

Sam was also excited about the trip because she would get to see Sara's parents' paintings. They were both art teachers. They not only painted still lifes and landscapes, but lots of Bible scenes, too.

Sara nodded. "It'll be neat to take a drive through the countryside, too. If it's this warm, we won't even need jackets!"

The next morning, though, the weather wasn't quite as nice. In fact, Sara, Sam and Maria had barely left home for school before it started raining. Hard! And it never stopped all day long. By the time school was out, the water was so deep on the streets and sidewalks that Sonya couldn't even use her wheelchair. Her dad had to come and carry her from the building to their van. Maria's and Sam's dads, who were mechanics at the same auto shop, found themselves busier than ever towing cars that stalled in the fast-rising water.

That afternoon, Sara's mom and dad listened to the radio as they packed up their paintings. "We're in for a real storm, folks," said the announcer. "Look for at least another foot of rain tonight, with flash floods possible at any time. The highway patrol is recommending that people stay home, or if you must go out, be very careful!"

Mrs. Fields sighed. "I'm really nervous about going out! But the road to Midland is on pretty high ground. And we do need to be ready for the exhibit opening tomorrow."

"We'll be careful," her husband replied. "I'll keep the radio on for road closings. We can triple-wrap all the paintings in thick plastic so they won't get wet when we take them out of the car, and tie ropes around them just to be sure. Girls," he added, addressing Sara and Sam, "make sure you take your boots, raincoats, the whole works. You, too, Tony," he nodded to Sara's big brother. "Just in case."

They loaded the car inside the dry garage, so that part was easy. But driving on the Circleville streets, and even out on the highway, was slow going. Even with their windshield wipers on at full speed, Mr. Fields could barely see to drive. Some cars hydroplaned —

skidding right across the asphalt. Here and there, red lights flashed as police cars and tow trucks tried to help drivers in trouble.

"Look!" Sara cried, as they passed a tow truck in the process of latching on to a car. "It's from the SuperService. Must be your dad, Sam."

Sam waved out the window, but it was raining much too hard to see anybody. Or hardly anything else, for that matter.

"Bob," Sara's mom said hesitantly, "I'm getting nervous about this. Maybe we should wait until tomorrow morning."

Her husband sighed. "No, we have classes to teach then, remember? But we just have a few miles farther to go. We'll pass by Lucky Lake and Crawdad Creek. But they're a couple of miles away. And we won't be near any rivers that might flood."

Then suddenly a river ran right into them! Not a real river, but swirling, churning, yellow water as far as the eye could see. It cascaded over fields, over the highway and over the lower trunks of the trees that lined the road. "Well, that settles it," Sara's dad decided. "I'm turning around and heading back. It'll be getting dark soon, and I sure don't want to be out here then!"

But as he started to turn the van around, a big surge of water suddenly rolled by. Just like that, the water was as high as their car doors. The van's motor sputtered and died. Right afterward, another big wave of water came crashing in. Now it was halfway up their doors!

"We're sitting ducks, Dad!" Tony cried. "We've got to get out of here."

"There's a big tree right beside us!" Sara added. "We could climb the tree and take the paintings with us, then stash them up on a big branch — if we move fast enough."

"And," her dad added grimly, "if we aren't swept away getting out of the car. Tony, take one of the ropes off one of those paintings. We'll use it to hold onto as we get out. I think I still have a first aid kit and a flashlight in here," he said as he reached under his seat. "There. I've got them. Okay, everyone make sure your boots are on. Then get out. NOW!"

Sam didn't think she'd ever prayed so hard in her whole life. She was terrified. But she knew that she had to be strong and brave and not panic. *Please help us, dear God!* she asked over and over as she pushed open a door and water rushed into the van.

It seemed an eternity later, but it was really just a few minutes until they were all safely up in the tree. Basketball player Tony's long arms and legs were a big help in boosting up everyone and the paintings.

As they crouched in the tree, Sam watched water lapping at the roof of the van, high above where her head had just been. Mr. Fields led them all in prayer. Then he recited, "'The eternal God is your refuge.' He's right here with us to protect us."

With the dark clouds, blinding rain and late

hour, the Fields family and Sam seemed plunged in darkness. Would anyone find them? Could anything possibly get worse?

Just then, Sam heard a faint meow. It was a scared cat — somewhere up in their tree!

· Good News · from God's Word

Here is the Bible story of someone else who asked God for help in time of trouble.

A Sick Woman's Plea

FROM MATTHEW 9:18-22

As Jesus traveled from place to place, people rushed to be near Him. They wanted to hear Him preach and teach about God. They asked Him questions. They begged Him to heal their sick friends and family members.

Jesus loved everyone. He wanted to help them all. Because He was God's Son, He had the power to help.

One day Jesus sailed across the Sea of Galilee to an area called Capernaum. People saw Him coming. By the time His boat had landed, a large crowd was already waiting for Him.

As Jesus began teaching the people, an important leader knelt at His feet. "My little girl is dying!" he cried. "Please come and save her."

There was someone else in the crowd who needed help, too: a very sick woman. For years she had been bleeding and none of her doctors knew how to help her. In fact, she had gone to so many doctors that she spent all of her money on them, but she kept getting sicker instead of better.

"I know Jesus could help me!" she told herself. "But I'm not worthy to bother Him. I'm not important like this synagogue leader. Since He's the Son of God, though, maybe I don't have to waste His time talking to me. Maybe I could just touch His clothes and be healed that way."

So she squeezed her way through the crowd and touched His cloak as softly as she could. Instantly, she was healed!

Immediately, Jesus turned around. "Who touched Me?" he asked.

"Goodness, Jesus!" cried His disciples. "This crowd is so big, everyone's touching you!"

The woman realized that Jesus knew what she had done. She fell at His feet, confessed and begged forgiveness.

But Jesus wasn't angry. He was glad. "Daughter, your faith has healed you," He said. "Go in peace."

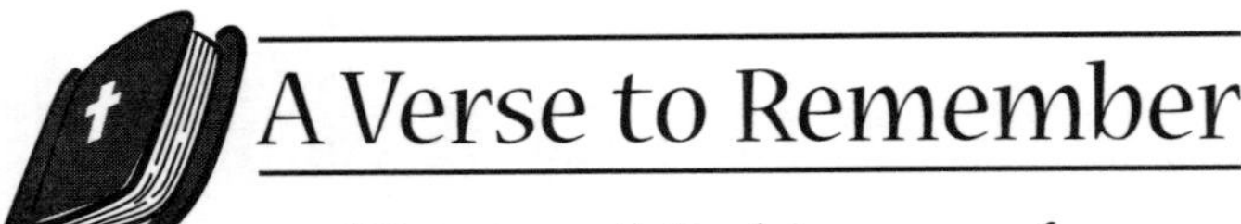

A Verse to Remember

The eternal God is your refuge.

— Deuteronomy 33:27

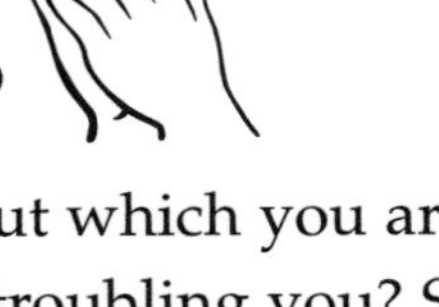

What About You?

Is there something about which you are really concerned? Something that's troubling you? Someone for whom you feel sorry? Write your prayer request below with today's date. Then pray for that person or situation. And keep on praying until God answers your prayer.

Request: ______________________________

Date: ______________________________

Request: ______________________________

Date: ______________________________

Request: ______________________________

Date: ______________________________

First Aid Kit

Every house and car should have a first aid kit. If your family doesn't have one in both places already, ask your parents if you may make one (you can also buy ready-made first aid kits). Start with what you already have on hand, then add to your kit as you are able (see the list below). Put everything in a metal or plastic container to keep it safe and watertight. Store a flashlight and fresh batteries with it. Also, take a first aid class so you can learn how to use the supplies.

Include in your first aid kit: antiseptic wipes (in individual packages); adhesive bandages; gauze; elastic bandage with clasps; triangular bandage; antibiotic cream; antiseptic spray; ointment for insect bites and stings; aspirin; eye drops; antacid liquid, tablets or gum; cough drops; scissors; first-aid tape; disposable gloves; cold and/or hot instant compresses; tweezers; thermometer; and first aid manual.

Joyful Easter Puzzle

Add the Secret Letter "A" for "asking God's help" to space 19 of the puzzle on page 26.

Chapter 3

Waiting and Hoping

Sam, Sara and her family all clung to the rough, slippery branches and to each other. Every few minutes, Mr. Fields shot his flashlight's beam downward to check the water level, which was steadily rising higher and higher. Then he would direct the flashlight upward and out to let any rescuers know they were there.

That's when they saw the kitten high above them. They tried to coax the shivering creature down. However, it was too terrified to move.

After about an hour, the rain slowed, then it finally stopped altogether. So did the wind. But the water kept rising. The Fields family and Sam were all so cold and wet, even with their boots and raincoats, that they could hardly keep from shaking.

Then they heard a helicopter motor. Sara's dad waved his flashlight around wildly. The helicopter turned its big searchlight in their direction, almost blinding them all!

"Yeah!" they all shouted, waving to the plane. "Here we are!"

The helicopter searchlight flashed on and off, as if in response to them. Then the helicopter crew tried lowering a rope ladder, but it kept getting caught in the trees. Finally, after a few minutes of trying the helicopter just flew off.

Sam could hardly keep from crying as she watched the helicopter's lights get farther and farther away.

"Don't worry," Mr. Fields said. "They'll be back, now that they know where we are. They'll probably come by boat." He started singing, "Row, Row, Row Your Boat."

That was such a silly thing to do, the others had to laugh. They all joined in to break the tension. Next they sang "Michael, Row Your Boat Ashore," and several other old camp songs. A full moon came out behind the dark clouds.

This is almost fun! Sam thought. *If we don't all drown, that is!*

The singing seemed to relax the kitten. Tony reached one of his long arms up to the kitten's branch. It stuck out a paw to touch his fingers. Then he managed to grab the kitten and slip it inside his jacket. The kitten trembled and meowed for a while, then it fell asleep.

"Lights!" Sara shouted suddenly. "Here comes our rescue boat! And the helicopter, too!"

The motor boat was large enough to hold all of them, plus the paintings. Sam felt a little seasick as the boat churned up and down through the powerful waves. But she was thankful for the strong arms that helped her down from the tree and the skillful rescue crew that brought them at last to safety.

After calling the Pearsons from Midland to let them know Sam was safe, and to ask them to check on Tank, their dog, the Fields family got ready to spend the night on the art gallery floor. Sam made a quick call to Shannon.

"Absolutely not!" cried Shannon's mom when she heard they were staying at the gallery. "You girls can spend the night with our family. And our pastor's family has extra room for Sara's parents. Tony can stay over at our youth pastor Bill's place."

When Shannon and Mrs. Hendricks arrived to get everyone moved for the night, Tony showed them the kitten inside his jacket. "Poor little darling!" Mrs. Hendricks exclaimed. "I'd better keep him at my house tonight. I'll dry him off and get him some food. You see, the youth pastor's landlady has a mean, old tomcat. He might be rough on a tiny kitten."

Shannon's mom found pajamas and robes for Sara and Sam. While they took hot showers to warm up, she cooked soup and cornbread.

Sam and Sara had fun trying to make a ponytail out of Shannon's tumble of short brown, natural curls. Then they all snuggled down with quilts around them to watch the TV news.

"Look!" Sam shouted. "That's us! See…up that tree! They must have had a camera in the helicopter!"

"Talk about a bad hair day!" Sara giggled. "We belong in a horror movie!"

The three girls crawled under the covers of their makeshift beds on the living room floor. Then Mrs. Hendricks read aloud to them from her Bible about Naomi and all the kind friends God sent to help her. After she was done reading, she asked, "What would you girls like to sing?"

Sara thought for a moment. She didn't usually sing at bedtime devotions, but she sure liked the idea! "What about the 'Doxology'? You know, that one we sing at church sometimes at the end of the service?"

Sam nodded as she sang the first line, "Praise God from whom all blessings flow."

Shannon smiled. "Good choice. Without God's help, we would never have made it tonight."

After they sang, Mrs. Hendricks turned off the lights. Sam could hear her bustling around in the kitchen, feeding and petting the orphaned kitten. She made him a little bed and a litter box. "Good night," she told him as she turned off the light and went upstairs.

Sam was too excited to sleep. Apparently the little kitten was, too. After a while, she heard, "Meow! Meow!" then the pitter-patter of little paws. Finally, the warm, furry and cuddly kitten snuggled up in Sam's ponytail and started purring contentedly. Within minutes, they were both sound asleep.

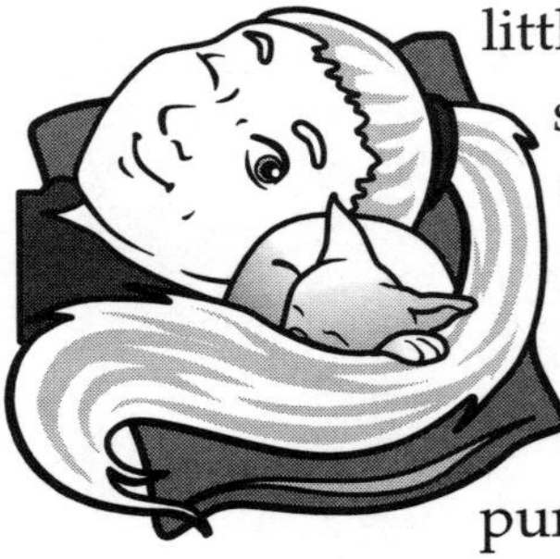

· Good News · from God's Word

Here is the Bible story Mrs. Hendricks read.

Naomi's Loving Friends

FROM THE BOOK OF RUTH

Naomi was a very happy woman. She and her husband and two sons. They also had a new home in the land of Moab.

Then Naomi's husband died. But her sons grew up and married two wonderful young women. They helped Naomi to be happy again. But then her sons died, too.

Naomi was heartbroken. "I have no one now," she sobbed. "I'm old and all alone."

"You have us," said her daughters-in-law.

"We'll all live together and help you."

"No," sighed Naomi. "I'm going back to my hometown, Bethlehem. You girls go back to your families, too. I don't want you to be sad and alone like me."

"I love you!" Ruth said. "If you're going away from here, I'm going with you."

And she did. She helped Naomi make a new home in Bethlehem. Naomi become reacquainted with her old friends, made new ones and found a whole new life. Ruth even married, but her new family still included Naomi.

When Ruth gave birth to baby Obed, Naomi was his caretaker. All of Naomi's women friends came to visit her and see the darling baby. They were glad that Naomi's life was happy again. Naomi was glad for her new family and friends as well!

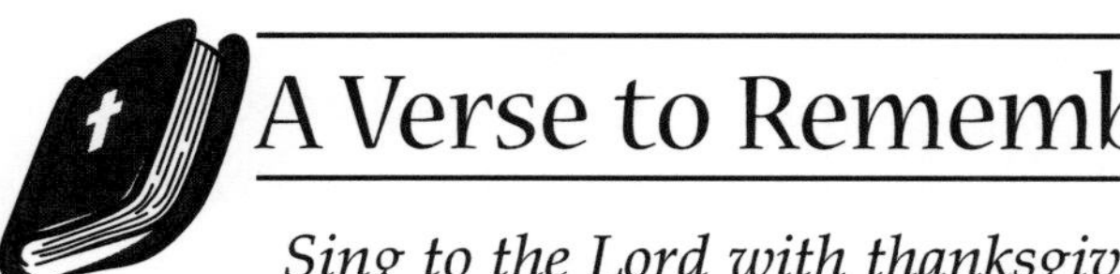

A Verse to Remember

Sing to the Lord with thanksgiving.

— ***Psalm 147:7***

Thanks a Lot 

Here's a silly thank-you game you and your PTs can play.

What to Do

1. Get in a circle. The first player should say, "Thank you, thank you for all you do. Now I'll give a gift to you."
2. Then that player should name an object, which can be as silly as you want, and another player's name. For example: "I give an elephant to Mandy."
3. Immediately, Mandy should say the same two lines the first player said. Then she should name a gift which starts with the last letter of the first gift (in the above example, it would start with "t," the last letter in "elephant") and the name of the next player. For example: "I give an elephant to Mandy and a tricycle to Sarah."
4 Players can go in order around the circle or jump around so no one will know who will be next. The last player should say, "Thanks to everyone of you. I'm awfully glad this game is through!"

2-4-6-8

It is always good to send a thank you card to people in appreciation for what they have done for you. Be sure to write in it exactly for what you are thankful. In other words, if Aunt Marie sent you a new video game, don't just say, "Thanks for my gift." Say, "Thanks for my new video game. It's so much fun to play!"

It's fun to make your own, personalized thank-you cards, too. You can use the pattern on the next page, or design one of your own. This card is based on the school cheer: "2-4-6-8, who do we appreciate?"

What You Need

- pattern
- white or colored paper
- scissors
- crayons or markers
- stickers (optional)

What to Do

1. Trace or copy the pattern onto white or colored paper.
2. Cut out the card.
3. Fold it twice, card style, as indicated by the dashed lines on the pattern.
4. Color the card with crayons or markers. Add stickers if you want.
5. Be sure to write the recipient's name inside the card and why you appreciate him or her. Then sign your own name.

Joyful Easter Puzzle

Add the Secret Letter "A" for "appreciating others" to space 12 of the puzzle on page 26.

2-4-6-8-

2nd Fold

1st Fold

Who do we appreciate?

____

write name here

because ________________________

Thank you!

____

sign your name

Chapter 4

God's Gift of Trees

The next morning, the flood was the main story on all of the TV news programs. A picture of Sara's family and Sam in a tree over the water was featured on the front page of the newspaper.

But capturing the girls' attention at Shannon's

house was another part of the story: the adorable kitten, who tumbled on their laps. "I hope we can keep him," Sara said. "Well, what I really mean is, I hope I can keep him. I know Tony loves him a lot, but Tank is really his dog. I want my own pet."

Shannon took her turn petting the ball of fluff. "What would you name him?" asked Sam.

" 'Stormy,' because God saved him — and us! — from the storm!"

The sun was already shining brightly, with no more downpours forecast. And there was more good news: although the water level continued to rise all night, it was now falling. All the stranded motorists had been rescued, and the towns of Midland and Circleville, which had become marooned "islands" with the water around them, were both safe and dry.

However, many farms in the countryside near Lucky Lake had been flooded. Those families were taken to rescue missions and other shelters, including the one in Circleville. Thankfully, there were no deaths.

And no school in the county for the rest of the week!

"Yeah!" cried all the PTs when they heard the news.

The exhibit's grand opening was postponed until the flood subsided. Fortunately, the thick plastic wrapped around the plastic had kept the paintings watertight through the whole weather adventure.

At the gallery, Mr. Fields set up an easel displaying the picture from the morning's newspaper. The picture showed not only the group huddled on the bare tree branches, but the awkward bundles of paintings as well. They titled this special part of the exhibit "God's Gift of Trees."

Then the Fields family and Sam all went with Shannon's family to help at the Midland homeless shelter. Extra beds for the flood victims had also been set up at Shannon's church.

"We're making room for them at Faith Church, too," Sam's mom said when Sam called to check in. "We've set up cots in most of the Sunday school rooms. Granny B.'s heading up the kitchen crew for them." Granny B. was the grandmother of another PT, LaToya Thomas.

Everyone was fine there, Mrs. Pearson reported, including the Fieldses' dog, Tank. They had brought him over to the Pearsons' house until the Fields family returned. He was having a ball playing with Sneezit, she said. Meanwhile, Sonya's, Sam's and Maria's dads were working around the clock at the SuperService station helping people with stalled cars and trucks.

"Your Sunday school teacher has her hands full helping down at the rescue mission," Mrs. Pearson added. "And you can't believe how many stranded animals have been brought in to our animal shelter. Horses, cows, sheep and pigs. You name it! Even aquariums." Then laughing, she added, "Can you imagine rescuing fish from a flood? Here, Petie wants to say something."

"Hurry home, Sam!" he cried as he grabbed

the phone from his mom. "I need you here. With only me here, Mom and Dad notice everything I do."

Sam laughed. She knew how mischievous Petie was. "But Petie, I have to wait until the water goes down more."

"Why? You can swim, can't you?"

Sam chuckled. But how would they get home, even when the roads were open again? After being under water, the Fieldses' van would have to be repaired before it could run again. If it ever could!

Two days later the county roads were reopened. Sam's Uncle Todd drove his SUV to Midland to pick up Sam and Sara's family. Sam's dad came along in the tow truck to pull the Fieldses' van.

On the way back, they stopped at the tree from where they had been rescued. Looking at the small patches of water here and there over the flat, soggy fields, it was hard to remember the terror they all felt that night. Tony sized up the huge, bare tree that had protected them all. "Wonder what kind of tree it is?" he said. "Oak, maybe?"

Mrs. Fields hugged the sturdy trunk and nodded. "Yes, it's a white oak, Tony. Thank You, God," she whispered softly as she rubbed her hand against the tree, "for allowing this tree to reach out its arms to us."

Mrs. Fields took pictures of the tree. Plus more pictures with Tony, Sam and Sara back up on the branches. *Boy, did that feel strange being in the tree again!* Sam thought as she worked her way back to the ground.

Then Sara's mom searched for some oak leaves and acorns in the deep, soggy grass at the foot of the tree. "For keepsakes," she said. "And inspiration."

The next week when the "God's Gift of Trees" exhibit opened at the Bon Jour Art Gallery, reporters and art critics from nearby towns and colleges poured in. They enjoyed the lush, rolling landscapes Mr. and Mrs. Fields had painted, especially those full of trees. A lot of praise was heaped on their still lifes and portraits.

But the center of attention was a display describing their night in the flood. A tape was available featuring people's memories from the flood, including little Stormy's plaintive meow.

Also, two special oil paintings and a print received a lot of notice. One of the new paintings by Mrs. Fields was of Noah and the animals emerging from the ark after the Flood. A gorgeous rainbow spread high above Noah's outreached arms as he thanked God for sparing them all.

The other showed Tony up in a large, bare oak tree. Water churned about in the blackness below as he reached up to a terrified kitten. It was titled, "Tree of Refuge."

To create the print, Mr. Fields had dipped an oak leaf in red paint and stamped it over and over again on a sheet of white foam board. The leaf prints together made the shape of a cross. Near the top he glued a "crown of thorns" made from acorn caps. It was titled "Tree of Life."

Sam was sure she had never seen such beautiful artwork in her life.

Sara — who had little Stormy on her shoulder playing with her red ponytails — agreed.

· Good News · from God's Word

The flood Sam and Sara faced was over in a few days. What if you were in one that lasted months? That's what happened to a family in the Bible.

Noah's Daughters-in-Law Show Gratitude

FROM GENESIS 6:9-9:17

You probably know that God instructed Noah to build a huge boat called an ark. It had to be huge, because it would hold two or more of all the world's land animals and birds, plus food to feed them all. And it needed to be watertight so it wouldn't sink.

It was hard work to find the trees and chop them down to build the ark. Then they had to put all of the pieces together to make a boat shape. But Noah wasn't alone. He had a wife and three sons. Then each of his sons married, making eight people altogether to help do God's work of getting the ark ready.

Imagine planning meals for all those people and animals for months! Imagine trying to do laundry in a rain storm without modern washers and dryers.

Imagine all the nooks and crannies on the ark that needed scrubbing. Plus, they had to clean up after the animals and feed them.

Noah's daughters-in-law didn't have any children yet, so they didn't have to worry about little kids falling overboard. But as the days and weeks and months went by, they must have longed to set their feet on solid ground again, and have normal homes and families.

When the Flood was finally over, people and animals were free to leave the ark and begin their new lives. They built an altar and sacrificed on it, showing their gratitude to God for protecting them through the flood.

Then God put a rainbow in the sky for them as a promise to care for them, and to never have such a huge flood again.

A Verse to Remember

Always giving thanks to God the Father for everything, in the name of our Lord Jesus Christ.

— Ephesians 5:20

Up a Tree?

Here's a quiz about some of the trees mentioned in the Bible. See if you can match the trees below with the list of clues below and on the next page. Check your answers on page 188.

A. pomegranate B. myrtle C. ebony

D. sycamore E. cedar F. oak G. fig

H. apple I. almond's nut J. willow

1. Of trees, this evergreen's a leader.
   Tall and fragrant is the __________.

2. By rivers, like a tall green pillow
   Grows the graceful weeping __________.

3. Angels once to Abraham spoke
   Beneath an acorn-producing __________.

4. Its fruit is sweet; its leaves are big
(Eve wore some once!). It is the __________.

5. As red as the cheeks of a girl named Janet
Is the delicious _____________.

6. This wood is as black as can be.
That's why we call it ____________.

7. Its spreading branches gave room for
Zacchaeus, who climbed a _____________.

8. With lush green leaves and blossoms fertile,
God's people liked the graceful __________.

9. Its blooms are pink and fragrant, but
Even better is the ____________.

10. As lovely as an outdoor chapel
(With yummy fruit) is, yes, the ___________.

Joyful Easter Puzzle

Add the Secret Letter "S" for "sincerely grateful" to space 9 of the puzzle on page 26.

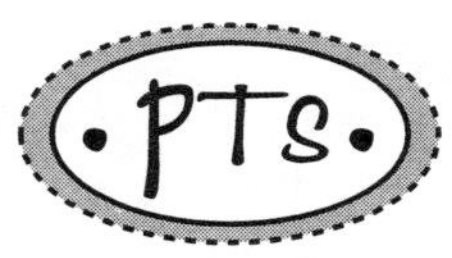

Chapter 5

Music to My Ears

By the time the flood was over, everyone was ready to get back to school — homework, tests and all. "I never thought I'd miss this place," Ric confided to Sonya, as he sat down beside her in science class. "But guess what? I did."

Just then, Mrs. Eldridge said she had an announcement to make. Everyone perked up. Class is so much more fun since Mrs. Eldridge came back from being sick, Sonya thought. Mr. Andover, their substitute teacher, tried hard but it just wasn't the same.

"Class," she began, "the countywide science fair will be held at Midland next Thursday. Our school will be represented by the first, second and third place winners in last fall's science fair, including four from this class: Maria and Le with their project on insects and LaToya and Sara's one on sunflowers."

"Oh, I'm so excited!" Maria said out loud. "I wish everyone could go."

Their teacher laughed. "Don't worry, I have something for them, too: a brand-new project!"

Amid groans, she explained, "This one is guaranteed to be fun because each of you will be picking your own subject. You can team up if you wish. For your assignment, think of a question to which you always wanted to know the answer, and see if you can find that answer."

"Any question at all?" Ric asked.

"Well, nothing illegal, of course. It should be something you can complete in a week, because your report is due next Friday. And it should have something to do with science. For instance, wanting to know if Sylvester will someday eat Tweetie Bird is not exactly scientific, okay?

"Those of you involved in the countywide fair are welcome to participate, too. But I think you'll find yourself quite busy until that fair is over. So the rest of you take a minute to think about what you want to do. Or bounce your ideas off someone else."

Ric turned to Sonya. "Hey, want to team up like we did for Winter Camp?"

She laughed. "But I don't have a clue what to team up to do!"

"Well, I do. I mean, did you ever wonder if the shapes of trees have anything to do with the shapes of their leaves or their seeds or fruit?"

"Are you kidding?" Sonya giggled. "Come on, Ric. That doesn't rank too high on the excitement scale, you know."

"Yeah, but it might be interesting. I mean, unless you have a better idea."

She thought for a minute. "Actually, I do. You play the sax like a pro. But exactly how does each hole in your saxophone know to make a different sound? How does it all work?"

"Oh, that's easy. You see..." Ric got a sheepish look on his face. "Hey, I guess I don't know after all. We'll find out. That'll be our project!"

Just then Kevin poked him in the back. "That's a great idea. You know, each of the drums I play has a different type of head on it and different types of sides. And they all make different sounds. Some even make notes. How do they do it? Maybe I'll copy you guys and find out what I can about that."

"No fair!" LaToya interrupted. "I'm stuck with my old sunflower project. I'd much rather learn how guitar strings work."

Sara chimed in. "And now that I have Stormy, I'd like to find out how cats purr. What will you research, Sam?"

Sam shrugged. She didn't have any ideas.

Of course, she did have a lot of questions about life, such as what she'd be when she grew up, and what it would be like in high school. But she sure wasn't going to find all that out in just one week.

"I dunno," she sighed. "Guess I'd better pray about it."

Saturday afternoon Sam took Sneezit for a walk in the Bark Park. The wind whistled like music through the newly-leafing trees. Birds were singing everywhere. Some of last year's leaves rustled underfoot. *What a wonderful world God has made!* she thought.

Sunday morning her Sunday school class at Faith Church studied Michal, King Saul's daughter.

"Michal admired young David's bravery," Miss Kotter, their teacher, said. "And why not? He was a real hero! But she knew about him even before he killed that giant, for David had been called from his shepherd work to play and sing for King Saul. His music must have filled the whole palace! Many of David's songs were probably praises to God because he later wrote most of the book of Psalms by himself. What a privilege we have to come to church and sing songs of praise to God, too."

That morning in church, Sam noticed that the hymns seemed to ring from floor to ceiling. At Zone 56 that evening, as they all gathered around their praise band, Sam felt like jumping for joy. Music was so powerful! It lifted her right up to God!

Sam decided that music would be the focus of her science project. *Maybe I could interview people and see why they like to sing or hear music,* she thought as she planned her strategy.

Sam started with the PTs. Then she asked her family and other friends, including all of the little kids she knew. She asked Ma Jones, Miss Kotter's friend, and some of the other elderly people she had met on their visits to the nursing home. She asked the music director at Faith Church and the church musicians. She even called in to a Christian music radio show and asked the D.J.

That Thursday was a great day for the kids at the countywide science fair. The Madison group came back with a blue ribbon for Maria and Le's project on insects. "Now you're eligible to go on to the state science fair," Mrs. Eldridge told them.

Friday was a fun day, too. Sonya and Ric displayed a chart on how a saxophone works. Then Ric played his sax to demonstrate what they were talking about. Kevin did the same on his drums. Other students did studies on how a hummingbird's wings work, why dogs turn around before they lie down, why people yawn when they get sleepy and many other questions.

As for Sam, some of the reasons people told her for enjoying music were: "I like the rhythm," "it's fun" or "stirring" or "romantic" or "bouncy" or "sad." But they all agreed that music helped them express what they felt in their own hearts.

To prove her point, Sam asked Sara to sing Madison's school song. By the second phrase, everyone had stood up, clapping and singing along. Kevin and Ric even joined in on the drums and sax. Now that was music they could all appreciate!

· Good News · from God's Word

Here is the Bible story Sam's class studied.

Michal's Love for a Singer

FROM 1 SAMUEL 16:14-18:29

Michal was a princess. Her father, Saul, was king of Israel. She had a sister, Merab and a brother, Jonathan.

Michal wasn't happy because her father wasn't happy. He was unhappy because he had sinned against God. He refused to confess his sins and get right with Him. Finally, his helpers looked for a musician to sing and play for him. They hoped the music would make him feel better. That's how they found David

David was the youngest of eight sons. His big brothers thought they were too important to take care of the family sheep. So they gave that chore to David.

But he didn't mind. He loved the animals. He grew strong defending them against bears and other dangers with his bare hands. Besides, sitting under trees while the sheep ate grass gave him lots of time to make up songs and sing them.

He especially loved to sing about God. He played on a harp as he sang — one small enough to carry around with him out in the fields.

When David came to the palace in Jerusalem, he was glad to meet the king's family. But mostly he was glad to help his king. For each time he played his harp and sang, King Saul did feel much better.

Soon Michal fell in love with David. He didn't know it, though. Later, David killed a giant that threatened God's people. Everyone finally saw him as a national hero as well as a young musician. After that, he and Michal got married!

A Verse to Remember

Sing and make music
in your heart to the Lord.

— Ephesians 5:19

Bible Praise Time

Music is mentioned many times in the Bible, including in the passages listed below. Fill in the blank in each rhyming clue on the with the correct persons or instruments on the next page. Forgot or aren't sure? Check out the Bible passages for answers, then see page 188.

1. Seven times they marched around Jericho-town. Then the ________ blew and the walls fell down.
   (Joshua 6:15,20)

2. Miriam, safely across the Red Sea, played a ________ to thank God for setting them free.
   (Exodus 15:20-21)

3. When King Saul was troubled, and couldn't find peace, David played on his ________, and Saul's bad moods would cease.
   (1 Samuel 16:23)

4. On the walls of Jerusalem, once more restored, marched two ________ of singers, in praise to the Lord.
   (Nehemiah 12:31)

5. To tell about Christ, without love, Paul makes clear, turns off folks like a ________ banged loud in their ear.
   (1 Corinthians 13:1)

6. That first Christmas night, some poor shepherds heard a choir of bright ________ announce the glad word. (Luke 2:13-14)

7. "You must worship my statue," Nebuchadnezzar did say, " when ________ of musical instruments play." (Daniel 3:1-5)

8. While he sat with his sheep, he'd sing and play. In our Bibles are David's ________ today. (The Book of Psalms)

9. We can praise God the entire day through, with psalms and ________ and spiritual songs, too. (Ephesians 5:19)

10. Can't sing or play any musical part? You still can make music deep down in your ________. (Ephesians 5:19)

A. all kinds B. heart C. cymbal D. hymns

E. psalms F. angels (company) G. trumpets

H. harp I. choirs J. timbrel (tambourine)

Joyful Easter Puzzle

Add the Secret Letter "E" for "exalting God's name" to space 2 of the puzzle on page 26.

Chapter 6

Wearin' of the Green

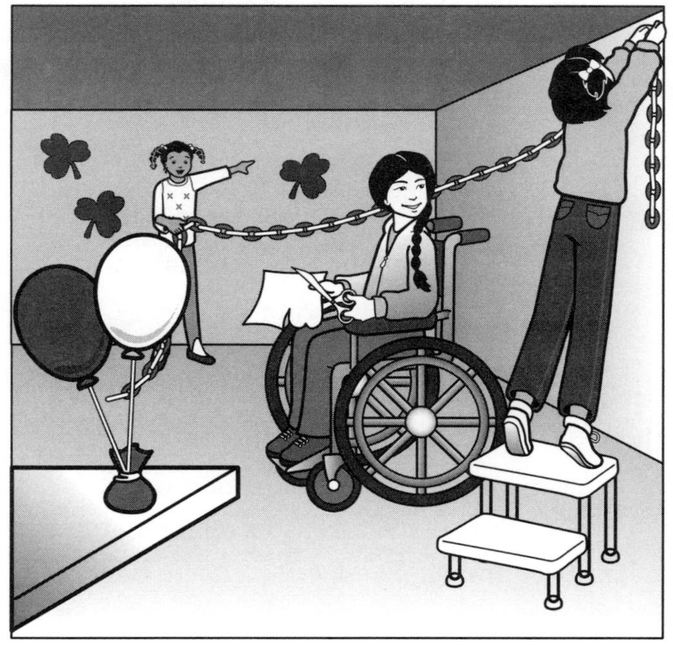

"Let's have a 'Paddy' party!" Kevin suggested one Sunday evening at Zone 56. "For next Saturday night. March 17th is practically here already."

"Sounds great!" agreed several of the other Zone 56 members.

Ric Romero made a face. This was his first time

at their regular Sunday evening get-together. "A paddy what? You mean, paddleball, as in Ping-Pong? Or…"

Sonya laughed. "As in St. Patrick's Day, silly. You know, 'wearin' of the green' and all that."

Sara raised her hand. "Let's invite the Midland kids to join us. We had such a great time over at their church for the praise night, even with the rain."

Brittany nodded. "And we can do everything in green — even the food."

"Even the food?" Kevin pretended to be shocked. "I don't know about green burgers and hot dogs. Sounds like something from the back of the fridge!"

Since the time was so short, they started planning immediately. Pastor Andy checked the Faith Church calendar, then called Pastor Bill at the Midland church. Everyone got on one committee or another: transportation, food, games, decorating and music.

"Hey, great party idea!" Sam's new Midland friend Shannon said when Sam called to tell her. "I can hardly wait for us all to get together again. What if our group brings some CDs and plans half the games?"

By 7:00 the next Saturday evening, the Zone 56 room had been transformed. Green crepe paper streamers, green balloons, green plastic tablecloths, green punch, green programs on the folding chairs, pots of blooming shamrocks — there was green everywhere! Especially on the Zone 56 members themselves!

Sonya had braided green ribbons into her long, black ponytail. Brittany wore new green pants and a green top. LaToya had dyed one of her sweatshirts a bright shade of green. Maria wore a new necklace with shamrocks on it.

But the one everyone noticed was Ric. As in Ric Romero. Not only had he applied green food coloring to his spiked hair, but his face and hands and arms were bright green as well.

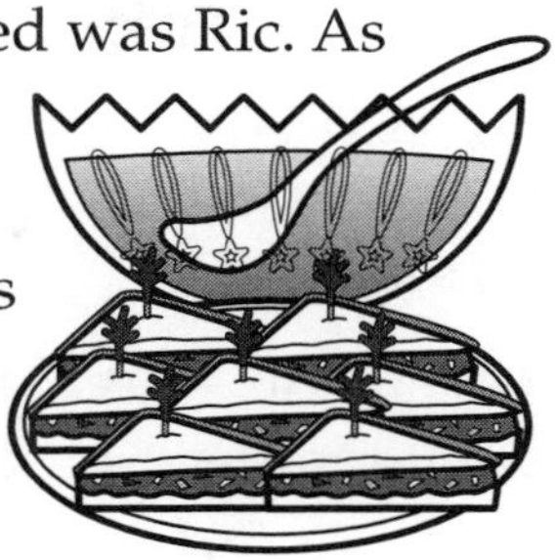

"Wow, Ric!" kids said to his face. But behind his back they whispered, "Gross! Like some slimy monster from the swamp." Indeed, Ric's "slime" was soon rubbing off on chairs and walls and clothes. Even on his food!

After lots of fun games and refreshments — including "paddy" cakes, lime sherbet punch and "green eggs and ham" (deviled eggs and deviled ham sandwiches, with a bit of green food coloring) — everyone sang some praise songs. Then Pastor Andy stood up in front of the group.

"Okay, kids," he began, "why are we all here?"

"Because we're not somewhere else?" joked Brian.

"St. Patrick's Day!" Le shouted.

"Right, and who was St. Patrick?"

Ric waved one green arm. "Some Irish dude."

"Okay," their youth pastor continued. "Know anything else about him?"

"Uh, he kicked the snakes out of Ireland?" someone else ventured.

"Actually, there were never any there. But he did something even more remarkable. He was a rich boy who became a slave who became a runaway who became a missionary who brought the Gospel of Jesus to pagan Ireland."

Then Pastor Andy told about the wealthy 15-year-old named Maewyn who lived in England under Roman rule, about 400 A.D. His father was a Christian nobleman, but young Maewyn wasn't really interested in the church himself. He went to school, but he wasn't interested in that, either. He would rather have fun with his pals.

Unfortunately, one day pirates invaded his town. The next thing Maewyn knew, he'd been sold as a slave to some Irish hog raisers. They thought it was a joke to have a nobleman's son out working with their pigs. So they mockingly called him "Patrick," which means "nobleman."

"Suddenly this teenager's whole life changed from goofing off to extreme exhaustion," Pastor Andy said. "He was miserable. But he noticed that his new owners were miserable, too. Even though Ireland was beautiful and green, the people lived in mud huts. They had no stores, no schools, no churches. Their pagan priests were very cruel. Their religion was cruel, too.

"While he worked with the pigs, Patrick had lots of time to think. He thought about his loving parents and the other loving members of his home church. He remembered some Bible verses he'd been forced to memorize. He didn't have a Bible, but he could think about those verses. He realized how much he needed God and how wonderful faith in Christ was. So he began praying, asking God to forgive him and to help him get back home.

"God did help Patrick escape — first to France, then back to England. But he didn't stay home safe and sound. Remembering those sad people in Ireland, he went back to them. They were amazed that he would risk his life for them. But when they saw Jesus' love for them shining through his life, they began turning to Jesus, too.

"One way St. Patrick taught was by using the three-part green clover leaf to teach about the Trinity: God the Father, God the Son and God the Holy Spirit. Eventually, he helped most of Ireland become Christians, all because he was willing to love and help even those who had made him a slave."

When he finished, the room was very quiet. Even later, when everyone was busy cleaning up and calling good-bye to each other, Ric stayed quiet. Finally, he got Pastor Andy alone. "You know, I'm sure green like St. Patrick on the outside," he said. "But could you tell me a little more about how to be like him on the inside?"

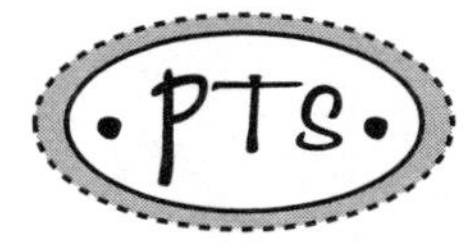

· Good News · from God's Word

Here are some more people who put Christ first in their lives.

Mothers Bringing Children to Jesus

from Matthew 19:13-15

Everyone was excited. There was a wonderful man traveling around the land telling people about God. His name was Jesus.

"He is a good teacher," some people said.

"He is the Messiah," said others.

"He is the Son of God," still others believed.

Some women watched Jesus as He preached and talked with people. They saw that He was good and kind and loving. Just being around Him was a blessing!

"Oh, if only our little children could meet

Jesus!" they cried. "Maybe He could help them love God, too."

So the women bundled up their children and started off to see Jesus.

It wasn't hard to know where to find Him. There were great crowds of people listening to Jesus' words there. People begged for Him to heal them. Cranky Pharisees wanted to argue with Jesus. His disciples tried to control all the "traffic."

The women worked their way through the crowd. They had their arms full of babies and toddlers. More little children held onto their skirts and hands. "We're almost there!" the mothers encouraged them. "Soon you'll be able to meet the most wonderful person in the world: Jesus!"

But as they got close to Him, His disciples stopped them. They looked at the babies sucking their thumbs and the small children with sticky hands. "Jesus doesn't have time for babysitting!" the disciples scolded. "He's busy doing important work."

Yet Jesus loved little children, just as He loved the grown-ups. "No, come!" He called. He grabbed the children up in His arms. He held them and blessed them and prayed for them.

A Verse to Remember

Let your light shine before men.

— Matthew 5:16

What About You?

Someone once said, "What you are speaks so loudly I can't hear what you say." Think about some kids you know. Maybe some guy is always putting others down. Maybe some girl is constantly telling people what a good Christian she is — but then she often gossips or criticizes others. We judge such people by their actions, don't we? Maybe we even call them hypocrites (people who say one thing but do another).

Make sure you let Jesus shine through your life every moment possible. When you goof up, confess, and ask Him to help you do better next time.

Eating of the Green

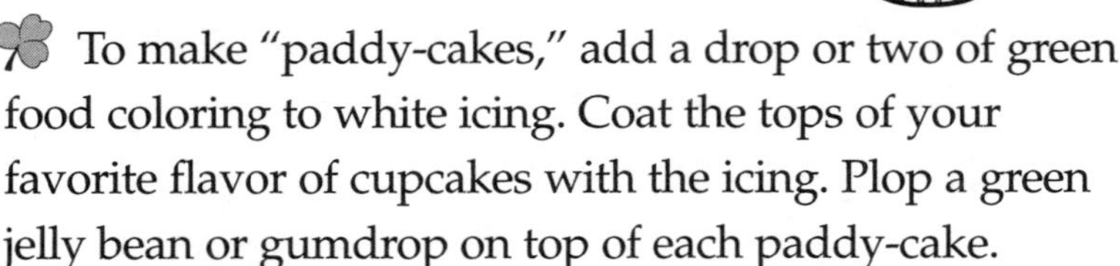

Want to throw a St. Patrick's Day party? Here are some fun tips for great, green eats and drinks:

- To make "paddy-cakes," add a drop or two of green food coloring to white icing. Coat the tops of your favorite flavor of cupcakes with the icing. Plop a green jelly bean or gumdrop on top of each paddy-cake.

- For "shamrock-y roads," cover small cookies (round or shapes) with green icing or white icing and green sprinkles. Scoop a dish of rocky road ice cream for each person, then stick three cookies in the top of each one.

☘ For "leprechaun juice" or "paddy punch," pour green drink mix, lemon-lime soda or frozen juice over lime sherbet. Add ginger ale and fresh mint leaves for a real taste sensation!

☘ Salads are already green! Shred and toss plain lettuce or add fresh spinach, mint leaves, celery, cucumbers, avocados — or whatever green veggie you like best.

☘ If you serve hot dogs or hamburgers, see if you can find a bottle of the new, green-colored ketchup. Or instead, serve plenty of pickle relish and pickle slices.

☘ Some people are allergic to food coloring, so if you add green coloring to any food, make all your guests aware of it before they start nibbling.

☘ Double duty: you can use some of these same green foods for a spring or summer party, or serve them with red-colored dishes at Christmas time.

Joyful Easter Puzzle

Add the Secret Letter "L" for "letting Jesus shine through" to space 16 of the puzzle on page 26.

Chapter 7

April Fool?

Maria sat down at the kitchen table and took all her school books out of her backpack. Setting them on the table, she opened up her social studies book to page 137. Then she opened her school binder. Starting with a fresh piece of notebook paper, she carefully wrote: "What I've Learned About My Family."

This was the new project Mr. Talley had given their social studies class that day. It was due the Friday before Mother's Day.

The first thing Mr. Talley said to do was make a family tree with all the aunts and uncles and grandparents and such that they knew about. Any names they didn't know they were to research. So Maria carefully made up a form like the family tree in her book and started to fill in the blanks.

"Grandpapa: José Moreno. Grandmama: Maria Moreno. She's the one I'm named after. Grandpapa: Ricardo Gonzalez. Grandmama..."

Just then her little brother Juan ran into the room. "Maria!" he screamed. "Come quick! Lolita fell off her scooter and is hurt bad."

Maria jumped up so quickly her papers and books flew everywhere. "Where is she?" she cried

Juan started to say something, but then he started giggling so hard he could barely stand up. "April fools!" he shouted.

"Oh, Juan, that was awful! That was a terrible thing to do!" Maria was so furious she almost burst into tears. "Besides, April 1st isn't until tomorrow. That's when we have April Fools' Day. Just wait until I tell Mama on you!"

Maria stormed into the kitchen to do just that, but Mrs. Moreno was on the phone with her own mother. They were talking in Spanish. When she saw Maria, she turned around and spoke in English. "Oh, Maria! Come say 'hi' to your Grandmama Gonzalez."

The last thing in the world Maria wanted to do right then was to be nice to someone. But she loved her grandmother. Grandmama Gonzalez was a short, plump woman with dark, sparkling eyes. All her life she had worked very hard. She worked in fields and raised eight children. But she was the sweetest person Maria ever met, and she was a great cook!

"*Hola*, Grandmama!" she said into the phone.

"Maria, dear," her grandmother said in Spanish. "Guess what? Your grandfather and I are coming to visit you over Easter vacation. All the way from Texas! I sure hope you like my enchiladas as much as you used to!"

Of course, Maria was thrilled at that. Not only did she love her grandparents, but maybe they could help her fill out the missing names in her family tree!

She could hardly wait to tell the PTs. She ran next door. "Sam, guess what?" she called as she ran up to the door.

But Petie opened it, not Sam. "Where's your sis?" Maria asked.

Petie looked very sad. "I don't know," he sighed. "We haven't seen her all afternoon."

"What?" Maria said with alarm.

Just then Sam ran into the room. "Hi, Maria," she said. "What's up?"

"April fools!" Petie giggled. Then he ran out of the house, laughing.

Maria could hardly keep from running after him and bopping him on the head. "What's with these kids?" she stormed. "April Fools' Day isn't till tomorrow!"

"I guess they're practicing," Sam said. "Come on in. I'm working on my family project already. And guess what? Grandma and Grandpa Pearson are coming for Easter vacation."

"Well, guess what back?" Maria grinned. "Grandmama and Grandpapa Gonzalez are coming then, too! Is that great or what?"

But after she went back home to help her mom with dinner, Maria thought some more about Juan's and Petie's tricks. Pretty soon she was simmering again, right along with the big pot of soup she was stirring. Finally she burst out with, "Mama, I'm so mad! How dare Juan and Petie play tricks on me and scare me half to death! It's not right! I'm going to get them back! I want to teach them a lesson!"

Her mother looked up from the dough she was kneading. "Temper, temper," she said gently. Then she added, "Maria, they were just teasing you. You can't control them. But you can control someone else: you, and your own temper. Speaking of lessons, remember the one you told me about from Sunday school last week?"

"Yes, but…" Maria stopped. Last Sunday, Miss Kotter had told them a sad Bible story about a queen with such a terrible temper that she was ready to kill people who got in her way.

"But I can't help it if people make me angry,"

Maria shot back.

"You can't help what they do. But you can ask God to help you control your temper. When you want to shout at someone, smile instead. You'll be amazed at how much better both of you feel."

So instead of shouting back at her mother, Maria smiled. It was hard. But she did it. And the more she did it, the more she kept doing it!

· Good News · from God's Word

Here is the sad story Maria remembered.

Jezebel's Temper

FROM 1 KINGS 16:29-19:2

Jezebel was the Queen of Israel. But she didn't act like a queen. Yes, she was beautiful and she had gorgeous gowns to wear and fine palaces to live in. She also had servants everywhere to do her bidding. But she was spoiled and selfish and mean. Born a princess, she had gotten her own way her whole life. And when she didn't, her temper exploded. (Maybe you've met someone like that?) Because she was unhappy, everyone around her became unhappy, too.

Jezebel didn't worship God. She had her own idols and her own priests and her own places to worship. She soon had her husband, King Ahab, building temples to her idols and worshipping them, too. Because they influenced their country to sin against God, He sent a great drought on them. There was no rain for three long years! Jezebel was so angry at God's prophets that she killed as many of them as she could.

At the end of the drought, the prophet Elijah came to see King Ahab.

"This is all your fault!" Ahab stormed.

"No," said Elijah. "It your family's fault for turning against God. Bring 850 of your wife's pagan priests to Mt. Carmel. They'll all be on one side. I'll be on the other. Then we can see who the true God is."

The king, Elijah, the pagan priests and all the other people went to the mountain. Everyone, that is, except for Queen Jezebel. God rained fire down on Elijah's sacrifice and proved to the people that He was the true God. Then the people, who now believed, killed the false prophets.

Jezebel was so angry when she heard the news!

"I'll kill that Elijah!" she yelled.

She was like that for the rest of her life. Even though she knew the right way, she never apologized to people or confessed to God and asked Him to help her change. Instead, she became meaner and meaner. Finally, she died a horrible death.

Even today, you'll find her name in the dictionary, meaning "a shameless woman."

A Verse to Remember

In your anger do not sin.

— Ephesians 4:26

What About You?

Some people have a more difficult time with their tempers than others. If your mother, father or another family member has a quick temper and yells or hits without thinking, pray for them and ask your pastor or another adult friend to talk to them.

If you're the one with the quick temper, learn the old trick of counting to 10 before you blow up in anger. Then count to 10 again! Also, before you say something mean, think: "Is it true? Is it kind? Is it necessary?" Ask God to help you "bite your tongue" rather than just blowing up.

April Fools!

Here are some statements about the PTs. Which are true (T) and which are April Fool's jokes (AFJ)? Mark the correct answer for each one. Some facts are from this book, while others are from previous Ponytail Girls books. Check your answers on page 188.

1. Sonya's dog is named Cocky. T __ AFJ __
2. Ric Romero lives with his uncle. T __ AFJ __
3. Miss Kotter is a nurse. T __ AFJ __
4. Sara has a new kitten named Sassafras.

   T __ AFJ __
5. During the flood, Sam stayed in a palm tree.

   T __ AFJ __
6. Suzie is Sam's older cousin. T __ AFJ __
7. Sara's parents are artists. T __ AFJ __
8. LaToya's Granny B. is a football star.

   T __ AFJ __
9. Le plays the violin. T __ AFJ __
10. Brittany has a new pet gorilla. T __ AFJ __

Joyful Easter Puzzle

Add the Secret Letter "A" for "aware of our own shortcomings" to space 6 of the puzzle on page 26.

Chapter 8

A Not-So-Funny Bunny

Jenna Jenkins' little sister Katie came dancing home from school with a bag full of artwork. "Jenna! Mom!" she cried. "Look what I did! Oh, I love Easter!"

Katie dumped everything out onto the floor. "Look!" she shouted. "Didn't I do good? I've got Easter bunnies and Easter eggs and butterflies and flowers and everything!"

Grabbing the Easter bunny picture, she ran into the nursery and waved it in front of her twin baby sisters. "Look, Noel! Look, Holly! This is what Easter is all about!"

They cooed and reached for the brightly-colored paper.

Mrs. Jenkins was busy folding clean baby clothes and putting them away. "That is a lovely picture, Katie," she said. "But that's not really what Easter is all about. Easter is about Jesus coming alive again."

Katie's face fell. "Is not," she pouted. "It's about the Easter Bunny. And I want a big Easter basket this year so the Easter Bunny will put lots and lots of candy in it! So there!"

Jenna was worried. After dinner she stopped by the Pearsons'. "Sam," she asked, "is Petie all worked up about the Easter bunny? Katie's out of control!"

"Oh, I don't think so," Sam started to say. But just then, as if on cue, her little brother ran in to the room carrying a newspaper ad. "Sam, here's a picture of that totally cool Easter video I want. It's all about the Easter Bunny and Donald Duck and Superman!"

Sam's mouth flew open. "Wait a minute, kid. Easter's not about rabbits and comic books. It's about Jesus."

Petie shrugged. "Whatever. Anyway, do you think Mom will get it for me?"

Jenna and Sam stared at each other. Jenna shook

her head. "We'd better ask Miss Kotter about this!"

That Sunday, Faith Church was decorated with pots of palm plants. They weren't as tall as the palm trees used that first Palm Sunday when people cut down branches for Jesus' donkey to ride on. But seeing them made Jenna once again think of long ago when Jesus was here on the earth. *How wonderful it must have been to see and hear Him!* she thought.

In Sunday school class, she and Sam could hardly wait to talk to their teacher.

"Miss Kotter," Jenna said, "all Katie and Petie can think of is the Easter Bunny. How can we help them remember Easter is about Jesus instead?"

"Yeah," Maria added. "I've got the same problem with Juan and Ricardo and Lolita."

Miss Kotter smiled. "Well, why do you suppose the children think Easter's about a very generous animal instead of a very loving Savior?"

"Well..." Sam frowned. "Because that's what they see on TV and in the stores. And besides, the bunnies are cute and the candy tastes good."

Their teacher nodded. "Then let's try to give them something to see and do and hear and taste that will help them learn about Jesus instead. Remember your Christmas Camp?"

Le nodded. "But that took up a whole week. Besides, Easter vacation doesn't start until after Easter."

LaToya raised her hand. "We could have it at

my house again, but maybe a one-day camp instead of a week-long. We could call it a Hurray Day to honor Jesus. Maybe next Saturday after vacation's started."

"Check with your mother first," Miss Kotter said. "Then if it's okay with her, we can meet all morning or all afternoon. Whom should we invite?"

The girls decided to invite all the children who had come to Christmas Camp, plus some neighbor children and all the PTs' dogs. The "guest list" even included little Stormy, the kitten. And, of course, their mothers, fathers and everyone else in their families.

But they decided to definitely not invite the Easter Bunny. Not even with Donald Duck and Superman!

· Good News · from God's Word

Here is the Bible story of someone else who honored Jesus.

The Crippled Woman's Rejoicing

FROM LUKE 13:10-17

Have you ever seen people who are permanently bent over so badly that they can hardly see what's in front of them? It usually means they have a very serious spine problem. Some people are born like that, but others develop the problem as children or adults. Sometimes they do not get that way until they are elderly.

We don't know the age of this particular Bible

woman. She might have been the age of your grandmother or of your mother. But for 18 long years she had been bent over so badly that she couldn't even lift up her head. Eighteen years — that's longer than you have been alive!

Even though she could hardly walk, she always went to her synagogue for worship and prayer. That's where Jesus saw her one Sabbath. How sorry He felt for her!

"Come here," He said.

She could hardly move. But of course she came. She couldn't see Him because she was so bent over but she did want to be near Him, as everyone did.

"You are healed, woman," Jesus said. Then He touched her. And immediately she was healed!

"Praise God!" she shouted as she turned 'round and 'round with her brand-new body. Now she could see Jesus for real. Oh, how she loved Him! Only the Son of God could heal her like that!

But the synagogue leader was angry. "Here, here!" he scolded. "We're in God's house to hear His Word and pray, not to heal people. Go heal them another day of the week instead!"

But Jesus told him he was wrong. He explained that it was always the right day to do good things.

A Verse to Remember

They took palm branches and went out to meet him, shouting, "Hosanna!" "Blessed is he who comes in the name of the Lord!"

— John 12:13

What About You?

How do you like to honor Jesus? Maybe you wear a WWJD bracelet, or a sweatshirt with Scripture verses on it. Maybe you love to listen to Christian tapes and CDs. Great! But the best way of all to honor Him is with your heart and your life. If you haven't already made the decision to live for Him, are you ready now? If so, talk to your pastor, parents or Sunday school teacher. It's the best way possible to have Easter all year long!

On a Little Donkey

To help you remember the joy of the first Palm Sunday, copy the donkey picture on the next page onto another sheet of paper or white poster board. Leave the top half of the paper blank above the donkey. Now fold the sheet at that line. Cut out the donkey through both thicknesses of paper or cardboard beginning with the fold on one side, cutting down around the legs and ending at the fold on the other side. Your donkey should stand up.

You can glue on yarn or thread for mane and tail. For a Jesus figure to ride your donkey, use an old-fashioned clothespin (no metal spring). Add chenille wire arms. Glue on fabric scraps for clothes and bits of black felt or yarn for hair and beard. Put Him on the donkey to "ride." Snip the edges of green paper to make palm leaves.

Joyful Easter Puzzle

Add the Secret Letter "J" for "Jesus-honoring" to space 1 of the puzzle on page 26.

Hosanna!
Blessed is he
who comes in
the name of the
Lord!

Chapter 9

Hurray...or Forget It?

When Ric heard about the Hurray Day for kids, his face lit up. "Oh, cool! Can I come and help?" Sonya stared at him. "Uh, but, uh, well, it's just girls that do it, Ric. You know, just us PTs."

"Oh." His face fell. "I...I thought maybe you could use guys for games and stuff."

"You're right! Sara's big brother is going to help with that. You know Tony. He's that star basketball player from the high school. So, sure, would you like to help Tony? Is it a deal?"

He grinned. "Deal!"

The Hurray Day wasn't the only thing the PTs had to worry about that week.

Jenna's twin baby sisters became ill and her mother needed all the help she could get from Jenna and her sister Katie. Le's mom, a professional pianist, was busy every night with Easter concerts and special practices for Easter services at Faith Church. Brittany's parents, who were still in counseling, got into another argument over where they were going to spend Easter vacation.

Brittany spent a lot of time crying and talking and praying with the PTs over that! LaToya's dad had to work a lot of overtime at the supermarket stocking shelves because Easter was one of their busiest times. Miss Kotter was busy helping at the rescue mission every moment possible. And their friend Mrs. Greenleaf, an elderly lady who lived up the street from Sam and Maria, fell from her wheelchair. That kept everyone praying and worrying, too, until she got better.

Plus, everyone had homework every night. LaToya, who struggled with math, was especially concerned about another upcoming test.

"I don't know," LaToya sighed to Sam on the phone. "Maybe this Hurray Day's not such a good idea, after all. Maybe we should just call if off."

Sam suggested that LaToya call Miss Kotter. Miss Kotter said she would pray for LaToya. Then a few minutes later, she called LaToya back. "Well, I have a math test for you, too, young lady," she replied. "Got a pen handy? Good. Jot down the following numbers exactly as I tell you. Okay: 1,14, 25, 20, 8, 9, 14, 7. Got that?"

"Yes, but…"

"Good. Leave a space. Next is: 23, 15, 18, 20, 8. Got that?"

"Yes, but…"

"Leave another space. 4, 15, 9, 14, 7."

"Miss Kotter, if this is a phone number, I think it must be long distance."

"It's no phone number. And it's not 'phony' either," she laughed. "Keep going: Space, then 9, 19 and another space."

The gears in LaToya's head, already exhausted from studying for her test, were whirling. "Is this some kind of code?"

Her teacher laughed again. "You got it. 23, 15, 18, 20, 8, space. 4, 15, 9, 14, 7, space."

"I'm getting 'spaced out'!" LaToya protested with a laugh.

"We're almost done. Just four more: 23, 5, 12, 12. Got all that? This is the simplest code in the world. Number the alphabet from 1 for A to 26 for Z. Then decode what I just gave you and see if you still want to give up."

After she hung up the phone, LaToya carefully figured out the letter for each number. Then she decoded the message and read the letters in the right order. "Miss Kotter's right," she decided. "We're going ahead with Hurray Day. That's what God would want us to do." (*Can you figure out the coded message? See "You Can Count on It" at the end of this chapter to find out if you guessed right!*)

When Saturday finally arrived, everyone had a great time. Fortunately, the expected April showers held off long enough for all the dogs and kids to play outside. And Ric had a chance to get to know Sara's brother, Tony.

"Wow, Tony's grrreat!" he told Sonya, sounding like Tony the Tiger from the cereal commercial. "We're getting together one day next week for a little b-ball."

"Good luck. You're going to need it playing against Tony!"

Besides the fun, the snacks, the games and the songs, Granny B. got everyone together and told them the story of the first Easter week, from Palm Sunday to Good Friday to the empty tomb. Then they all watched a video that showed the same, awesome Bible story. But this wasn't just a story — it was fact!

"Wow!" Petie told Granny B. "That's better than any Easter basket. Jesus is sure somethin.' But I still like Easter candy, too, okay?"

Granny B. laughed. "Okay. In fact, I think there's some in the kitchen for everyone right now." So off ran Petie — she didn't need to tell him twice!

· Good News · from God's Word

Sometimes what we need to do seems so hard, we just want to give up. Maybe you have to study for a hard test, clean your room or help with the laundry. It would be a lot easier not to, but then you'd be sorry if you didn't! Here's a Bible story about a woman with a problem that required not giving up.

A Housewife Tackles a Difficult Job

FROM LUKE 15:8-10

Everywhere Jesus went He had stories to tell. Some of His listeners were eager to understand His messages. Others became angry. They didn't want to understand these teachings about God. They just wanted to argue and win the arguments. Did you ever meet someone like that?

One day a lot of people crowded around Jesus to hear Him. Most of them weren't serious religious types. They didn't have the right jobs or run around with the right crowd. At least, that's what some of the religious leaders thought.

"Look at that stupid Jesus!" the leaders muttered to themselves. "He doesn't even realize that these are terrible people He's talking to."

Of course they thought He couldn't hear them. And of course He could hear them! For He is God and knows everything!

So Jesus told another story, this time about a housekeeper. In Bible days, some houses had stone or tile floors. But many had only dirt floors, which were very difficult to keep clean.

Back then, when women got married they were often given shiny, silver coins as wedding presents to wear on their foreheads, under their scarves. So this woman may have had of them on her face, jangling and jingling whenever she moved. Or maybe she had put them away in a box or jar for safekeeping. In any case, these coins were the only "bank account" she had. She couldn't spend them on something silly. They were her "insurance" in case she really needed money some day.

One day the woman noticed that one coin was missing. She was horrified. It couldn't have gone too far, she reasoned. Maybe it was still somewhere in her house! But where? It was difficult to find anything on the dirt floor just by looking.

So she started a major housecleaning. How the dust and dirt must have filled the air when she swept that dirt floor! And then she had to dust the tops of everything else after the dirt settled on it!

But guess what? She found the coin! She was so excited and happy, she ran out and told all her neighbors so they could rejoice with her.

"That's just how happy God is when someone comes to Him," Jesus told His listeners when He finished the story. "And that means anyone…even those 'sinners' you religious people are criticizing!"

A Verse to Remember

She…works with eager hands.

— Proverbs 31:13

Joyful Easter Puzzle

Add the Secret Letter "E" for "enthusiastic" to space 10 of the puzzle on page 26.

You Can Count on It

This is the secret coded message Miss Kotter gave to LaToya. Lucky you: LaToya already figured out the key for you. Match the letters to the numbers to get the message. Check your answers on page 188.

Secret Code

1=A	2=B	3=C	4=D	5=E	
6=F	7=G	8=H	9=I	10=J	
11=K	12=L	13=M	14=N	15=O	
16=P	17=Q	18=R	19=S	20=T	
21=U	22=V	23=W	24=X	25=Y	26=Z

Secret Message

___ ___ ___ ___ ___ ___ ___ ___   ___ ___ ___ ___ ___

1 14 25 20 8 9 14 7   23 15 18 20 8

___ ___ ___ ___ ___   ___ ___

4 15 9 14 7   9 19

___ ___ ___ ___ ___   ___ ___ ___ ___ ___

23 15 18 20 8   4 15 9 14 7

___ ___ ___ ___

23 5 12 12

What does the message mean?

____

____

Chapter 10

A Day of Miracles

That Easter morning a few stars still glittered in the sky when Sam's family left the house bundled up in jackets and jeans. They were heading out to the Easter sunrise service by Lucky Lake.

As they drove along the quiet city streets in their van, Sam's dad said, "You know, this is the same time of day the women went to Jesus' tomb that first Easter morning, while it was still dark."

Riding out toward Lucky Lake, Sam realized she hadn't been on that road to Midland in the daytime since right after the big flood. How everything had changed! The old oak tree that saved them was leafing out, full of the hope and promise of a new spring. So were the other trees. Several of the fields they passed were newly plowed. And here and there in farmyards shone golden bursts of forsythia bushes, plus redbud and dogwood trees in full bloom. And…

"Look, Mom! Tulips!" Sam called out. "Ours haven't come up yet! I wonder why."

"Because Sneezit dug up the bulbs," her father laughed.

It was much chillier by the lake than it had been in the car, and Sam was glad for her jacket. She waved at the other PTs. What a good turnout! Even the park ranger was there with his family. Mr. Pearson thanked him again for saving little Suzie from drowning last summer.

When they began singing Easter hymns, Sam was also glad for the melodies from LaToya's guitar and Sonya's harmonica. It was hard enough for her to sing in tune when a piano or praise band was playing. With no music at all, she was hopeless!

As she looked up at the pines and willows around her, she remembered Pastor McConahan's message at the Good Friday service. He told how tree trunks had been chopped down and the bark taken off to make Jesus' cross so long ago. The long bottom log was set firmly down in the ground on the Hill of Calvary. Then Jesus carried the other huge log on His weary, bloody shoulders the long way to that hill. When He became too weak to go on, a man named Simon helped Him carry it.

Sam found it sad to think that the Creator of trees was crucified by parts of those same trees. But Jesus did it because He loved her, she knew, and everyone else in the world. He loved them enough to die for them all!

Just as the service was over, the sun burst over the hills behind Lucky Lake, turning the water gold.

"Wow!" Petie cried. "This has been some Easter. What do we do the rest of the day?"

But they didn't have to sit around worrying about that! Faith Church provided hot coffee, cocoa and doughnuts for people to linger after the service. Then everyone headed back home for breakfast and to dress for church.

"Hey, I just came home from church!" Petie protested while Mrs. Pearson pulled his new pants and shirt from the closet for him.

Yet once they reached Faith Church, he was as excited to be there as his big sister was. After just seeing everyone in jackets and sweats at Lucky Lake, Sam hardly recognized her classmates. "Ooo, I love everyone's new spring clothes!" she said as she admired the PTs' Easter dresses.

In Sunday school, Miss Kotter told them the story of the first Easter morning, and how Salome,

Mary Magdalene and some other women came to the tomb. "But what they found inside was the most wonderful thing to find in a tomb you can imagine," she said. "What they found inside was absolutely nothing. It was empty! Because…"

Her class finished the sentence for her: "Jesus arose from the dead!" they all cried at once.

Another miracle awaited them: a standing-room-only sanctuary. It was jam-packed with what Granny B. called "folks with two-day religion: Easter and Christmas being the only two days!" But Granny B. was glad to have people come to God's house anytime, just as she always welcomed people to her own home any time.

Sam and Le finally found a place to squeeze in the back row where Sonya could park her wheelchair in the aisle beside the pew. Sam noticed that the man next to her didn't quite fit in with the others in the church. He had a long, gray ponytail and a long, gray beard with a shiny bald top in between. He was wearing a suit jacket, but with jeans, sneakers, a plaid flannel shirt and a bright red tie.

The man looked very uncomfortable. Sam saw that he didn't even know how to look up songs in the hymnbook. But then she saw that a boy sitting on the other side of him helped him. A boy who looked like…

It was Ric! This must be Ric's uncle, she decided. Ric had mentioned that his uncle had never been to church in his whole life! And here he was. Another miracle, Sam thought excitedly.

Sam felt ashamed for looking only at the man's clothes and judging him for it. *Forgive me, dear Father*, she prayed. Help Ric's uncle see Your love. And please do another miracle in his life — a miracle of salvation!

· Good News · from God's Word

This is the Bible story Sam's class studied that Easter morning.

Salome's Joy in the Impossible

FROM MARK 16:1-7

Salome was proud of her two sons, James and John. They were prosperous fishermen like their father, Zebedee, and partners with Peter and Andrew.

They loved God and wanted to serve Him. In fact, they were two of Jesus' disciples!

Salome was almost too proud of her sons. She wanted Jesus to make them His very top rulers over all the other disciples in His "kingdom." But Jesus helped her see that the kingdom He would rule over is the kingdom of the heart, not of armies and wealth.

As her sons became closer and closer to Jesus, Salome got closer to Him, too. She joined other women to help Jesus and His disciples by cooking for them and serving them. That way she could also be closer to her own beloved sons.

Salome was at the cross on that bitterly sad Friday when Jesus was crucified. She also came to the tomb that marvelously joyful first Easter morning to discover that it was empty. He was alive! He rose from the dead! Oh, miracle of miracles! He proved that He was indeed God's Son!

Salome also rejoiced later to see both her sons become great leaders for Jesus — not of an earthly kingdom, but of His church. John wrote five books of the New Testament: John; 1, 2 and 3 John; and Revelation. James was such a prominent leader that King Herod Agrippa finally had him killed. Even though Salome grieved for James, she was thankful that God could use her sons for His glory.

A Verse to Remember

God … raised Christ from the dead.

— 1 Corinthians 15:15

Joyful Easter Puzzle

Add the Secret Letter "O" for "open to miracles" to space 8 of the puzzle to page 26.

A Real Cross-word Puzzle

The puzzle on the next page explains why Jesus died on a cross for us long ago. Begin with the X at the top of the cross. Cross it out. Skip the next letter. Then cross out the last letter in that row. In the next row, skip the O and R and cross out the K. Keep going, crossing out every other letter. Copy the remaining letters in order on the spaces below. You'll find part of a very familiar Bible verse. The answer is on page 188.

___ ___ ___   ___ ___ ___   ___ ___

___ ___ ___ ___ ___ ___   ___ ___ ___

___ ___ ___ ___ ___   ___ ___ ___ ___   ___ ___

___ ___ ___ ___   ___ ___ ___   ___ ___ ___

___ ___ ___   ___ ___ ___ ___   ___ ___ ___!

Do you remember the rest of this verse? If not, turn to John 3:16 in your Bible.

					X	F	Y					
					O	K	R					
					T	G	J					
					O	L	D					
					V	S	Y					
O	B	L	N	O	X	V	G	E	K	D	P	T
C	H	A	E	B	W	C	O	D	R	E	L	F
D	G	T	H	H	V	A	I	T	J	H	K	E
					L	G	M					
					A	N	V					
					O	E	P					
					H	Q	I					
					R	S	S					
					O	T	N					
					U	E	V					
					A	W	N					
					X	D	Y					
					O	Z	N					
					A	L	B					
					Y	C	S					
					D	O	E					
					N	F	!					

Chapter 11

It's a Family Thing

Petie pushed so hard against the window trying to see out through the rain, his nose was squashed flat. "I think I see them! No, it's a truck. Maybe this is them!"

"A watched pot never boils, kiddo," Mrs. Pearson reminded him. "They'll be here just as soon as possible. Are you sure your room is picked up?

Remember, that's where your grandparents will be staying."

"Uh-huh. Why doesn't it stop raining? I don't like rain. I want to show Grandma and Grandpa how good I can ride my bike and skate and do wheelies on my scooter. It's spring break! It's not supposed to rain!"

Sam brushed the feather duster across the top of the piano. She had already dusted it once, but she wanted to make sure everything was perfect for her grandparents. "I hope Grandma remembers to bring some pictures for my school project," she said to her mom.

Mrs. Pearson sniffed the air and ran into the kitchen. "And I hope my cake didn't scorch!" she cried as she opened the oven door.

It didn't. And her grandparents arrived right on time. In Petie's room, the two twin beds were pushed together to make one big one for them. Mrs. Pearson had put a little cot for Petie in that room, too, which Petie liked because he could have his grandparents all to himself, at least for a while!

Dinner was yummy, with roast beef and mashed potatoes, string beans and a salad. Uncle Todd, Aunt Caitlin and Suzie showed up just in time for dessert, which was one of Mrs. Pearson's luscious cakes. Except this cake was unusual. As she served it, she said it was called "Tomato Soup Cake," but that it was "a soup you can eat with a fork." That sounded absolutely strange, but it was absolutely de-lish!

"We'll be by tomorrow for a longer visit," Uncle Todd said as they left.

After the dishes were done, everyone sat around

the living room telling stories and jokes.

"Could I help you hang up your clothes, Grandma?" Sam asked.

She laughed. "Actually, dear, we brought very few clothes. Let me show you what I did bring." Back in the bedroom, she laid out the suitcases on Petie's bed and opened them."

"Yeah, pictures!" Sam cried. "And letters! And look, a 'family tree' — already done up! Oh, Grandma! You're the greatest! Who's that cute girl in the old-fashioned clothes? And what is she doing at that funny desk?"

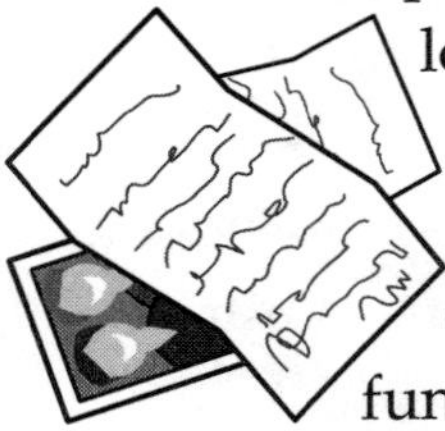

"Well, honestly, Sam! That's me! That's a special drawing table. I used it when I went to design school. Didn't you know about that?"

Sam's mouth flew open. "You're kidding! What did you design?"

"Clothes. Women's, mostly. After I graduated from design school I lived in New York for a while, designing fashion lines for firms. But I got homesick. I was too much in love with your handsome grandfather, you know. So I went back home to Michigan.

"But here," she said as she held out a portfolio, "are some of my designs."

The clothes looked like something out of an old movie. But the artwork was great. "Oh, we've got to show these to Sara's parents!" Sam exclaimed. "They're artists, too, you know."

Down in the basement, Petie was showing his grandpa his new inline skates. He zoomed around the rec room with Sneezit barking wildly at his heels.

"Tomorrow, Dad," Mr. Pearson said to his father, "I'll take you down to see our new SuperService station and meet my new boss. Pedro Moreno next door works there, too. You know, you met him at Christmas."

"Oh, yes. Great guy. Loved how he was fixing up those old classic cars in his garage."

Sam fixed some hot spiced tea to take around to everyone. *What a wonderful family night,* she thought. *Just like in a painting or something. Thank you, God, for my loving family, she prayed. And for letting us all be together.*

But just then the phone rang. Sam answered it. "Is this the night number for SuperService?"

"Uh, yes. Dad, it's for you!" she called.

Her dad picked up the basement extension. "I'll be right there," he said hurriedly and he grabbed his jacket and rushed out the door. "Wait a minute, Joe," her grandfather called. "I'll go with you."

Mrs. Pearson ran outside into the rain after them. "Where are you going, Joe? Is it an emergency?"

"Yes!" he shouted back. "Some guy skidded off a bridge in the rain. He's been rushed to the hospital. I think his name is Max Romero."

Oh, no! Was that Ric's uncle? That guy who sat by Sam at church Sunday — the first day he had been in church in his entire life?

Grandma Pearson joined them in the living room. She and Sam and Mrs. Pearson all prayed together. Then Mrs. Pearson dialed Pastor McConahan's number. "Pastor," she said, "I'm sorry to bring bad news but…"

Oh, dear God! Sam prayed. *I love my family, but Ric loves his, too. Please take care of Max. He's the only family Ric has!*

· Good News · from God's Word

This is the Bible story Sam's class studied that Easter morning. This Bible story is also about a loving family: Jesus' family.

Mary's Joy in Her Family

from Matthew 12:46-50

Jesus was born the very first, marvelous Christmas night. His mother, Mary, and her husband, Joseph, were full of joy and wonder that first Christmas night. Joining them in the stable to worship Jesus were some shepherds, angels and eventually three wise men. Then Mary and Joseph took Jesus to the temple, where Anna and Simeon blessed Him. God told Joseph to flee to Egypt to protect Jesus, but later He instructed them to return home safely to Nazareth, where Jesus spent the rest of His childhood.

Mary and Joseph worked hard to be good parents for Jesus and for the rest of their children, who were born after Him. Everyone needed to help with the housework, plus do chores to help around Joseph's carpentry shop. Indeed, Jesus learned to be a good helper there, and He became a carpenter, too.

Then God called Jesus into the ministry. He couldn't be home with His family anymore. Instead, He traveled around with His disciples, preaching and teaching and healing the sick. Jesus never seemed to take a break. "He will be exhausted!" Mary cried. "Let's go bring Him home to rest a while before He gets sick."

So Mary and some of her other sons traveled from Nazareth to Capernaum, where Jesus was staying at that time. Today the trip would probably take 30 minutes or so in a car. But back then it probably took a couple of days walking or riding a donkey. It was easy to find Jesus because He was right in the middle of a huge crowd, as usual. What wasn't easy was getting through the crowd to see Him!

Finally word got through to Jesus: "Your mother and brothers are here to see you."

Was He glad to see His family? Of course! But before He hurried to see them, Jesus turned to those who believed in Him. "This is my real family," He said, "because anyone who does the will of our heavenly Father is My spiritual brother or sister."

What does that mean for you today? Well, if you believe in Jesus, you are God's child — and Jesus' sister, too! Isn't that wonderful?

A Verse to Remember

Whoever does the will of my Father in heaven is my brother and sister.

— Matthew 12:50

Family Night

When was the last time your family had a fun evening together? See if you can help your parents or grandparents plan one. You'll want to select games, snacks and other entertainment. Or maybe there's a good video all of you could enjoy together. Or get out family pictures and look at them together. For a special treat, try Mrs. Pearson's cake recipe on the next page. Be sure to ask an adult to help you with the oven.

Tomato Soup Cake

What You Need

- 2 cups all-purpose flour
- ½ teaspoon salt
- 1 teaspoon cinnamon
- ½ teaspoon nutmeg
- ½ teaspoon ground cloves
- 1 teaspoon baking soda
- 1 cup sugar
- 2 tablespoons butter or margarine, softened
- 1 can condensed tomato soup
- 1 cup nut pieces (such as walnuts)
- 1 cup raisins

What to Do

1. Preheat oven to 350 degrees.
2. Sift flour. Add salt, cinnamon, nutmeg, cloves and baking soda to flour, then sift again. Set aside.
3. Drop butter or margarine into large mixing bowl. Add sugar and mix until soft.
4. Slowly add flour mixture to sugar.
5. Stir in soup and keep stirring until smooth.
6. Stir in nuts and raisins.
7. Pour batter into a greased bundt or tube pan and bake for 45 minutes.
8. Allow cake to cool, then add frosting, if desired.

Joyful Easter Puzzle

Add the Secret Letter "L" for "loving one's family" to space 13 of the puzzle.

Chapter 12

Helping Hands and Hearts

The news went through Circleville like wildfire.

Ric Romero's Uncle Max, whom Ric lived with, had been in a serious accident. His car skidded off the road near Midland and went over a bridge. The highway patrol rushed him to Midland Memorial Hospital for emergency surgery. Then they had called Mr. Pearson to pull the smashed car from the creek bed and tow it in for repairs.

But what about Ric?

"We can't have him home alone," cried Mrs. Fields after Mrs. Pearson told her the tragic news. "He's much too young for that."

So Mr. Fields and Tony picked him up from his apartment. First they drove him to the hospital in Midland so he could see his uncle. Then they took him back to their house in Circleville. "You can stay here as long as you need," Mrs. Fields told him. "Tony's got bunk beds in his room. If you want, we can drop you by your place tomorrow to get your saxophone and bike and stuff. Fortunately, this is spring break, so at least you don't have to deal with school right now."

"How could God do this to us?" Ric sighed to Tony later that night. He reached over to scratch Tank's ears. Little Stormy snuggled up to him, too. "I mean, I was just starting to get with this church-thing. You know, talking to Pastor Andy and stuff. Even talked Uncle Max into coming to church with me on Easter. Man, that took some doing, too. He was totally against any kind of Christians. He said they are 'pie-in-the-sky'-ers, 'weirdoes' and 'fanatics.' But he came anyway. And he didn't even get drunk that night. First time that's ever happened."

"Do you think maybe he got drunk again tonight and that's what caused the wreck?"

Ric sighed. "I don't know. I hope not. But now…"

And his voice trailed off into silence.

Just then the phone rang. Tony answered it. It was Pastor Andy calling for Ric. "Want me to come by and see you, guy?"

"Naw, I'm cool. But look, could you find out how Uncle Max is doing and call me back?"

"I'll try. And, Ric, I'll be praying for him."

"Uh, me too. Yeah, me too."

LaToya's big sister, Tina, who was a student nurse at the Midland hospital, was the one who called back.

"Ric, I'm sorry to call so late. But Pastor Andy asked me to call you back and give you a report on your uncle. One of my classmates at nursing school, Tiffany, is working over here in the emergency room. She said it's a miracle your uncle isn't dead. One leg was broken badly and some ribs were crushed.

"The water in Crawdad Creek was running pretty high tonight with all that rain we've been having. He could easily have drowned. Tiffany said God must really have been looking out for him."

Ric started sniffling. "Thanks," he said weakly.

Meanwhile, Maria's grandparents had arrived for Easter vacation, too. When Maria heard about Ric's uncle the next day, her grandmother insisted on inviting both Tony and Ric over for one of her big Mexican feasts. But Tony and Ric took a "rain check" instead, because Ric wanted to see his uncle. Tony drove him over to Midland, along with Kevin and some of the other Zone 56 guys and Pastor Andy.

"I feel so helpless about it all," Sam confided

to her grandmother that afternoon. "I thought this was going to be the greatest vacation with you coming and all. And now…"

Her grandmother hugged her. Then she reached into one of her suitcases. "I brought along some sketch pads and watercolor paint sets for you. If I remember right, you used to like to design clothes, too. Maybe we can work together on some. Also," she pulled out a bag, "here's some software that will help you design clothes on your computer. You can scan in your sketches, add color, change lines and all the rest."

"Grandma! How did you learn about computers?"

Laughing, she responded, "Well, honey! I wasn't exactly born yesterday. Also, here's a list of some web sites for you to do more family research."

Sam looked them over. "Grandma, I see a nice, juicy 'A' in my future for this social studies project. Maybe an A+! Thanks for this list. I think I'll e-mail a copy of these sites to Miss Kotter. You know, her parents died when she was little and she had to grow up in an orphanage. She might like to research her family tree, too."

Just then the church secretary called for the church's prayer chain. Sam's parents were both at work, but she took the message to pray for Mr. Romero, and then called the next family on the list. Even though it was difficult to share bad news, it made Sam feel better to know that even when something terrible happened, Christians could all love and pray and work together to help.

· Good News · from God's Word

Here is a Bible story about other Christians encouraging each other.

Philip's Daughters Encourage Paul

FROM ACTS 21:8-9

We don't know when Philip became a Christian. But he was already a leader in the church right after Jesus ascended to heaven. In fact, he was elected as a deacon to help make sure the poor widows in the church had enough food to eat.

That was a very important responsibility, and Philip handled it very well. But he didn't stop there.

Every chance he got, he told people about His Savior, Jesus. And every day more and more people came to know the Lord.

The Jewish leaders didn't like that. The Roman rulers didn't, either. They began persecuting the Christians. They threw everyone they caught into jail. Others had to flee for their lives.

Philip ended up in Samaria. But instead of hiding out, he began preaching about Jesus. The people were so excited to hear the Gospel that they came in huge crowds to state their belief in Christ and be baptized. In fact, the crowds were so great that Peter and John came to help Philip. Philip even presented the Gospel to the treasurer of the Ethiopian empire and baptized him. After that, Philip traveled all over the country as an evangelist until he came to the city of Caesarea. From then on, he lived there. But he still traveled all over, telling the Good News of Jesus.

We don't know if Philip was already married when he moved there or not, but he soon had a large family. With a loving father like Philip to guide them, they all learned to love God's Word, to pray and to tell others about Jesus. In fact, four of his daughters were called prophetesses because they spoke God's Word in truth and power.

Years passed. Paul was coming to the end of his missionary journeys and was headed for Jerusalem. He stopped by Caesarea on the way and stayed for several days at Phillip's home. Something interesting happened during his visit. The great missionary Paul was accustomed to helping others by explaining God's

Word to them. Now he was helped by Philip's daughters, four young women who shared God's Word with him!

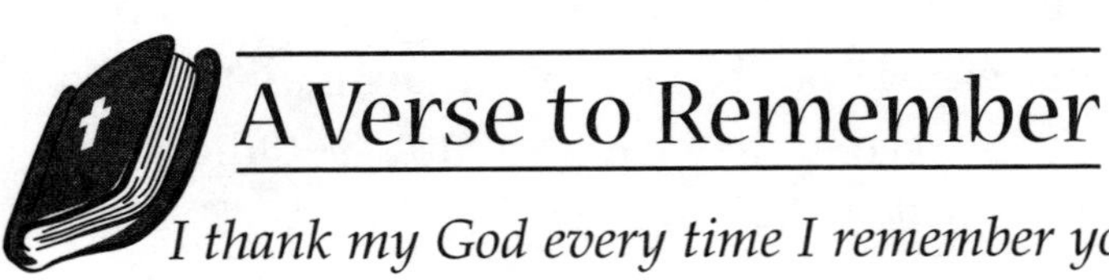

A Verse to Remember

I thank my God every time I remember you.

— Philippians 1:3

It's in There Somewhere!

Philip's daughters knew God's Word very well. How well do you know your Bible? Here's a quiz to help you find out. Cheating for this quiz is fair, because the more you look at your Bible or ask others for answers, the better you will know them! To check your answers, turn to page 188.

1. The four Gospels are:

   ______________ ______________

   ______________ ______________.

2. The first book of the Bible is ______________.

3. The book about leaving Egypt for the Promised Land is ___________.

4. The book of Judges is about courts in the United States. True ___ False ___

5. The book of Ruth is about a famous Russian queen. True ___ False ___

continued on next page...

6. The last book in the New Testament is ________________.

7. The book of Romans was written by Paul to people in ___________.

8. The title of which book in the Old Testament sounds like a math book? ______________

9. Which book is a "hymnal" written by David?

____

10. Which book is full of wise sayings?

____

11. Which book is the name of someone who was thrown into a lions' den? ______________

12. The title of which book means "very sad"?

____

13. Which book contains a whale of a tale?

____

14. The last book in the Old Testament is

___________.

15. Who wrote the first five books in the Old Testament? __________

Joyful Easter Puzzle

Add the Secret Letter "U" for "upholding others in prayer" to space 4 of the puzzle on page 26.

Chapter 13

Spring-ing Forth

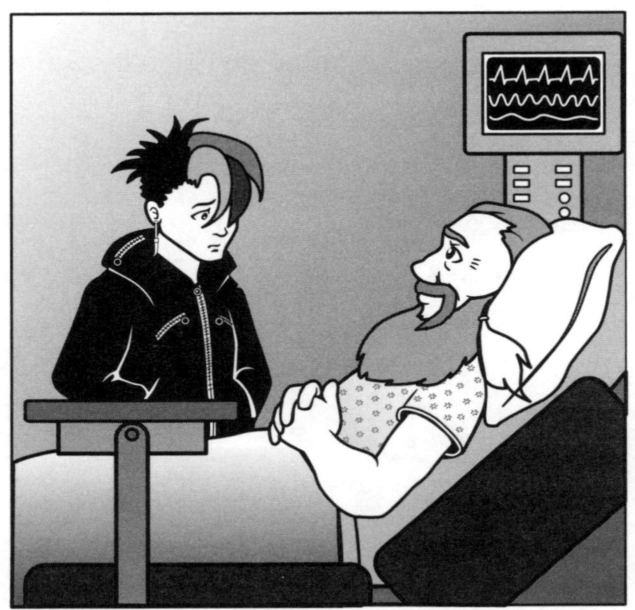

"What a gorgeous day!" Grandma Pearson remarked as she looked outside. "Look at Lena Moreno's daffodils and tulips! Really makes me want to plant a garden. Why, look at Maria's grandmother out there! I think that's just what she's doing!"

Sam nodded. "Maria's mom's already has radishes and lettuce coming up. But her grandmother's trying to get a lot more seeds going."

Sam stared at the sketch pad in front of her. "I

wish I could get this going, Grandma. I have such good ideas in my head. But I can't draw hands right. The arms look funny, too. Why can't I draw as well as you?"

"Oh, my dear!" her grandmother replied. "I'll let you in on a big secret. Yes, you want your figures to look attractive and halfway human. But when you're designing dresses, you really need to concentrate on the clothing. Maybe we can make a run to the bookstore later and pick you up a few books to help you get going. You can probably take classes in designing and merchandising when you're a little older, too, just as I did."

Sam's grandparents had been there four days. Four whole days! Spring vacation would soon be over. But how Sam had enjoyed their visit! Every day she and her grandma had pored over family pictures and letters while Sam took notes. She'd also been practicing her dress designing every day.

Something else good had happened during that time, too: Ric's Uncle Max was transferred to a regular room in the hospital. Next he would start physical therapy. After a few weeks, the casts would be off his ribs and legs.

He was happy about that. But he wasn't happy about his work.

"Uncle Max has always worked two jobs to pay the bills, Miss Kotter," Ric said as Sonya's dad drove a van full of Zone 56 members and Miss Kotter to the hospital to visit Ric's uncle. "Now there's no paycheck coming in. His insurance will cover most of the hospital bills, but what about fixing up his car? And what if his bosses lay him off? I mean, I can quit school and take a job down at Ben's Burgers or something. But it won't pay our rent. Man, this is a big mess."

"What kind of work does your uncle do, Ric?" Sonya asked.

"He's a paralegal. He works for lawyers. But there aren't many law firms around here."

Brittany broke in. "What about my dad's company? It's Gibraltar Insurance. Their headquarters are over in Summer City. They're not lawyers, but they have lawyers working for them. I bet they use para… whatever you called them…there, too."

"Really?" Ric almost smiled. "I'll tell him so he can check it out. I was also thinking about looking on the Internet for jobs for him."

The nurse gave Zone 56 permission to see Mr. Romero two at a time. They brought him flowers and wished him well. Then they left Ric alone with his uncle while they went back to the waiting room.

"Have you found out anything about your family on the Internet yet, Miss Kotter?" Sam asked.

Their teacher brightened. "Actually, yes. In a way. You know Ma Jones over at Whispering Pines, my substitute mom? I think we've located a couple of distant cousins on her father's side. As for me, I'm trying to find out who still might have the records for the Good Shepherd Orphanage where I lived, because it went out of business years ago. Has your grandmother been helping you out with your family tree project, Sam?"

"Oh, yes. She's even teaching me about dress design. Hey, Maria, I saw your grandmother out working in the garden before we left."

Maria nodded. "I'm amazed at all she knows about insects because of all those years working in fields. I'm taking notes so I can add that to our exhibit before the state science fair next week."

Ric was quiet when he joined them, but his face was glowing. "Well, guess what?" he said. "I found out Uncle Max wasn't drinking the night of the accident. The police made a note of that in their report. That will help on the car insurance. And guess what else? He said he'd never met church kooks as nice as you guys before."

Sonya grinned. "Well, maybe he should come to church more often and find out just how 'kooky' we are, right?"

Then Ric blurted out, "Mr. Silverhorse, do you know a good barber, someone who can do something with my spikes? And cover up my dyes? I'm tired of messing with it."

He never had a chance to answer — Brittany did it for him. "I do, Ric! The one Mom and I go to. I'll call for an appointment and then we can go together. Deal?"

He high-fived her. "Deal! I want a whole new look before school starts up again next week. 'Cause I think there's gonna be a lot of good, new stuff for the Romeros from here on out!"

· Good News · from God's Word

Like Sam, all the other PTs and their friends have been busy during Easter vacation learning new things. Jenna spent a lot of time learning to care for her new baby sisters. Le's mother taught her how to play some ancient Vietnamese musical instruments. Sara learned some new cheers to use for softball games. Sonya learned some Cherokee words from her father. LaToya took classes to help her get ready to try out for the gymnastics team. Here's a story from the Bible about someone else who wanted to learn something new, and where she went to learn it.

The Queen of Sheba's Amazing Visit

FROM 1 KINGS 10:1-13

In Solomon's day, Sheba was a great country. It ruled much of what is now called Arabia, and was famous for its shipping and caravan businesses. The people also built ingenious irrigation systems in the desert, many of which can still be seen today.

Because Solomon, as king of Israel, did a lot of shipping and trading, too, he probably did a lot of trade business with Sheba. Sheba's fleets traded in gold and apes, precious stones and spices, and all kinds of luxury merchandise. Everything Sheba sent Solomon's way, he bought. How was this possible?

That's what captured the interest of the queen of Sheba. She was, of course, rich. But apparently Solomon was richer! She was very wise, also. But everyone said Solomon was wiser. In fact, he was world-famous for all he knew.

"Well, I'll just see about that," she decided. "I'll go talk to him face-to-face and ask the trickiest questions I know as well as some to which I don't know the answers. That way I can find out how smart and rich and amazing this famous king really is!"

In Bible times, the head of one nation couldn't just pay a visit to the head of another nation whenever he or she felt like it. A meeting such as that took a lot of back-and-forth negotiation between the courts. Also, the queen would need a lot of soldiers and servants to travel with her, plus lots of expensive gifts. Even today, many arrangements are required to bring together leaders of two nations.

Solomon welcomed his important visitor. We don't know how old she was or whether she was attractive or not. But we do know she was self-confident, intelligent and eager to learn. She fired question after question at him, like in a TV quiz show! He just as quickly answered them all. Then she was led on a tour through his palace, through the temple and through the great scientific gardens he had built.

Finally, she said, "Everything people told me about your kingdom is true, King Solomon. But I couldn't believe it until I came and saw it with my own eyes! Praise be to God who has put you on this throne!"

Then she gave him all her gifts: gold, spices and precious gemstones. He gave her gifts as well. She returned home rejoicing, and much the wiser for her trip.

A Verse to Remember

Show me your ways, O Lord,
teach me your paths.

— Psalm 25:4

What About You?

Is there something you would like to learn? A new way to wear your hair? Or to speak Spanish? Or make good beef stew like your mom makes? Or hit the ball out of the park? Or something else? Whatever it is, write it on the next page with today's date:

____

____

Date: __________

What is it going to take for you to learn this new skill? Whatever it is, start right now to make a plan. Remember, the sooner you start, the sooner you will begin learning to use the interests God gives you. And the sooner you begin, the sooner you will succeed.

Nursery Nonsense

These familiar characters from nursery rhymes and fairy tales all need to learn something new. Choose a character from the list below to fill the blank in each statement. Have fun!

A. Cinderella
B. Quite contrary Mary
C. Sleeping Beauty
D. Nimble Jack
E. Little Boy Blue
F. Tom, the piper's son
G. Little Jack Horner
H. Little Bo Peep
I. Goldilocks
J. Beanstalk Jack
K. The farmer's wife
L. Little Miss Muffett

1. I need to learn how to keep track of my farm animals.

____

2. I need to learn how to stop stealing.

____

3. I need to learn how to not be afraid of spiders. ____

4. I need to learn how to stay out of other people's houses. ____

5. I need to learn how to grow beanstalks the regular size. ____

6. I need to learn to plant normal things in my garden. ____

7. I need to learn how to be nice to disabled mice. ____

8. I need to learn how to keep my shoes on. ____

9. I need to learn how to be safe around fire. ____

10. I need to learn how to stay awake when I'm on duty. ____

11. I need to learn how to have better table manners. ____

12. I need to learn how to check apples for safety. ____

Check your answers on page 189.

Joyful Easter Puzzle

Add the Secret Letter "E" for "eager to learn" to space 15 of the puzzle on page 26.

Chapter 14

Live and Learn

Sam could hardly believe her eyes. "Grandma! Look at this!" she cried, waving the morning paper as her poodle jumped up to see. "Out of the way, Sneezit!"

Sam's grandmother was busy packing suitcases to return home. She and Sam had carefully made copies of all the pictures and letters Grandma had brought. They had also gone to the bookstore and to an art supply store in Summer City to get Sam everything she needed to work on dress designs. So Sam already thought her Spring Break was as wonderful as could be. And now this!

Grandma Pearson looked up. Then she adjusted her glasses. "It's a design contest. I remember entering one when I was just your age up in Michigan. I won second prize for my age group, if I remember right."

"Oh, Grandma! Do you think I have any chance at all to win if I enter this one?"

"My dear, you have no chances at all if you don't. And your chances are even better if you work hard and do your best. By the way, if you need to send a sample of your design and not just a drawing, you'll have to sew it yourself. I understand LaToya's Granny B. is a great seamstress. Maybe she can help you."

Then she stood up. "If you don't mind, I'm going to take a quick nap before we leave for the airport."

As she quietly closed the bedroom door behind her, Sam decided she just had to share this great news with someone. Right now! It couldn't be her parents, since they were at work. And it couldn't be Maria or LaToya. Maria was helping her grandparents pack up to leave, too, while LaToya was finishing up her last day of gymnastics classes.

Instead, still holding onto the paper, Sam dashed over to Sara's house.

But Sara had gone with Brittany to cheerleading practice. Tony and Ric had gone back to the hospital to see Uncle Max. So Sam rushed over to Le's.

Le was busy listening to some Vietnamese music CDs. "I'm going to include a tape of samples with my family report," she said. "You know something? I never liked this kind of music. But now the more I study it, the more I like it. In fact, Mom and I are going to play some together for the next Vietnamese Christian concert. And little Nicholas and Michael are going to sing!"

Nicholas and Michael? For a moment, Sam had forgotten all about Dr. Phan's little boys. His wife had died, and now he was dating Le's mom. Le's dad, Daniel, had died years earlier. "Le, your mom and Dr. Phan have been dating since before Christmas. Do you think they're serious?"

Le looked wistful. "I guess so. I hope so. They really love each other. And I love those little boys. But my dad's been gone so long, it would be strange living with more than just my mom. I'd appreciate it if you'd keep my mom in your prayers, that she will know the right thing to do."

As for the design contest, Le said, "Great!" But obviously her mind was somewhere else. So Sam headed next for Sonya's.

Sonya was home. And she was thrilled about the contest, but not just for Sam. "I want to enter it, too!" she decided. "I mean, I'm not as good at drawing as you or Sara. But who better to design clothes for girls in wheelchairs than me? It's hard to find clothes that are comfortable and still look good!"

So she looked up the ad in her own newspaper. Then the girls read over the rules together and decided to be each other's support in entering the contest. Sonya would design clothes for girls with physical problems; Sam would come up with casual outfits that could go from sports to dinner or parties.

"Oh, guess what else I'm into?" Sonya added. "I've gotten onto the Internet and found out all kinds of stuff about the Cherokees. I think I'm going to ask Dad if we can go visit the old Cherokee lands in North Carolina or the Cherokee nation in Oklahoma during summer vacation. That way I can learn even more about my family."

That evening, after the Pearson and Moreno grandparents had left for home, Zone 56 held a fun night at the church. The high school kids even joined in. They munched popcorn while they watched silly, old black-and-white movies. The high-schoolers organized a "Guess the Baby" contest where everyone posted their baby pictures on the wall, then tried to figure out who grew up to be whom.

Tony didn't want anyone to see his baby pictures so he didn't bring one, but Sara found a way to sneak one in! When he saw it, his face turned almost as red as his hair. But, of course, the high school girls just cooed and told him what a cute baby he was.

"Look at that! I can't believe how girls think he's so cute," Sara said to Sam. "If they saw him first thing in the morning I bet they wouldn't be so in love!"

"If anyone saw me first thing in the morning they'd run the other way!" Sam laughed.

Pastor Andy gave a short talk, during which the PTs noticed Miss Kotter slipping in the back. With a good-looking guy! The PTs were surprised because they knew how heartbroken she had been when her last boyfriend broke up with her. After a short prayer,

Pastor Andy explained that he'd invited Miss Kotter and Evan Strauss, who worked with her at the computer software company, to answer questions about computers. As Miss Kotter and Mr. Strauss shared, they teased and laughed with each other, which made it a lot of fun for the listeners — except Pastor Andy, who wasn't smiling at all.

Sam nudged LaToya, then whispered, "Look at Pastor Andy. He's so serious. Do you think he's mad about something?"

"He's mad all right," LaToya whispered back as Miss Kotter and Mr. Strauss finished their talk. "Mad about Miss Kotter! I think he's jealous of this Evan guy!"

Sam leaned over excitedly to tell Sara the news, but she stopped abruptly when Ric solemnly asked Pastor Andy if he could speak. Sam almost didn't recognize Ric! His hair was all one color — brown instead of red or orange or purple — and it was cut short. He'd even done away with his earring and nose ring! As he stood, Ric looked around hesitantly. Everyone stared. A few gasped!

"You know," he said, "trying to change my life around is hard work. It's been even harder for Uncle Max. I mean, he's had years of experience doing the wrong stuff.

"I changed my hair and got rid of my piercings because I wanted to show on my outside that I've changed on the inside."

Ric stopped for a moment and smiled. "But I

might still get a cross earring," he said sheepishly.

"Anyway, I want to thank everyone for their help. And, uh, well, I thank God most of all. You know, my so-called Dad left when I was a little kid. It's great to know I've got an even better one now," he said nodding upward, "and that's God, my real Father. Thanks, Dad."

Ric got tears in his eyes. And so did just about everyone else in the room!

· Good News · from God's Word

There are two reasons hard work isn't much fun: one, it's hard; and two, it's work! But sometimes that's the only way to learn or achieve or do what needs to be done. This Bible story introduces someone who didn't mind a little hard work. Not when what she wanted to get done was so awesome!

Sheerah's Hard Work and Success

FROM 1 CHRONICLES 7:24

Joseph was a hard worker. He worked hard as a young teenager, taking messages and supplies from home to his brothers who were traveling around with the family flocks. He worked hard as a slave and prisoner in Egypt, doing work for his masters. Later, he was second in command of all of Egypt — a free, rich and wealthy man with all the right connections. Yet he still worked just as hard because he believed that was what God wanted him to do.

While living in Egypt, Joseph married. Later, he had two little boys. One of them was named Ephraim. These boys were born into great wealth. But they knew how to work hard, too. When Ephraim grew up, he married and had four boys and a girl. Her name was Sheerah. Two of those sons, sheep ranchers, were killed. The Bible says Ephraim was so sad he mourned for them for a long, long time.

We don't know much about the other two sons except that they, too, grew up and married and had children. And then their children had children. By then their people had been forced into slavery, so everyone had to work hard. Hundreds of years later, by the time they set out with Moses to cross the Red Sea to freedom, their descendents had grown to be thousands in number.

But the Bible does tell us something about

their sister, Sheerah. It tells us she built something: a city. Not just one city, three of them! She even named one of them after herself. Two of the cities crowned hilltops. They are still there today, thousands of years later, though they are now just villages.

More remarkably, Sheerah built these cities in Canaan where Joseph lived, although her family lived in Egypt. The Egyptian army protected Joseph's granddaughter while she was there. Even so, transportation of supplies must have been a problem.

All the other city founders mentioned in the Bible are men. It was hard then for women to own land, to employ helpers, to learn building skills and to do the work involved in erecting buildings. Not to mention finding the money to do it all with!

Maybe Sheerah's father, Ephraim, helped by giving her that money, or her grandfather Joseph. Or maybe it was her other grandfather, who was a very important priest. But she still had to do the hard work all by herself, just as you will have to work hard in life to succeed.

God doesn't want you to be lazy. He expects great things from you. And He can help you do them if you allow Him to be a part of your life.

A Verse to Remember

The people worked with all their heart.

— Nehemiah 4:6

From One PT to Another

What would you advise Le about her mother getting married again?

____

____

What would you tell Ric's Uncle Max?

____

What would Sonya need to keep in mind as she designs clothes for disabled girls?

____

Gone to Pot

Most Native American people, like the Cherokees, used pots and baskets. There are 25 simple pot shapes in the puzzle on the next page. Can you find them all? (Hint: Start at one end and color in each shape as you find it.) The solution is on page 189.

Joyful Easter Puzzle

Add the Secret Letter "H" for "hard-working" to space 11 of the puzzle on page 26.

Chapter 15

United We Stand, Divided We . . . Oops!

"Our first day back after spring break, and I'm tired already," Sonya griped that Monday on the way to school.

"Well, having that time off did help Le and me get ready for the statewide science fair Friday," Maria replied. "Mrs. Eldridge is going to drive us. The fair's in Riverton this year. That's such a long drive we'll have to go up there the evening before and stay in a hotel overnight. I'm so excited! I've never been to Riverton. And I've only stayed in a hotel once in my whole life."

"Well, don't worry. You and Le make a great team. Isn't it exciting about Ric? He not only acts better, he looks better. It's like he's all new."

Maria laughed. "Well, that's exactly the business God is in: making people new."

Just then Sam caught up with them. "Thought of any designs yet?" she asked Sonya. Then she and Sonya explained to Maria about the contest. "We're not going to work on the same ideas, but we'll help each other whenever we can."

That Thursday after school, all the PTs got together to give Maria and Le a big sendoff. For the trip, they gave each girl and Mrs. Eldridge a decorated bag of candy and snacks with each person's name and "Good Luck!" written on it.

After dinner that evening, Sara and LaToya got together in LaToya's room to practice a song for next Sunday at church. Meanwhile, Kevin, Josh, Ric and Brittany, who were all in the church praise band, gathered around Granny B. downstairs while she taught them some old Gospel songs, plus a little rhythm and blues for fun.

Brittany was embarrassed at how much better

the others played than she did. But she was determined to improve enough to play with them in church some Sunday. Her mother came with her every Sunday now. But her dad still stayed away. At least he still went to counseling sessions with Pastor McConahan.

Mr. Moreno's garage was noisy, too. He wasn't just tinkering on one of his old, classic cars. He was earnestly trying to get it running as soon as possible to replace Mr. Romero's car, which had been totaled in the wreck. The money the insurance company paid Uncle Max afterward not only wouldn't buy a new car, it wouldn't buy a decent used car. But Uncle Max certainly needed one, especially if he took a new job over in Summer City. So Pedro Moreno decided that by the time Max was ready to drive again, he would have him something ready to drive!

As for the other PTs, Jenna was babysitting Katie and the twins that evening while her parents went out for dinner. It was their first "date" in months. Sonya and Sam worked on their fashion designs. Mr. Silverhorse had driven Miss Kotter in his van to pick up Opal and Shirley at the train station. They were Ma Jones' long-lost cousins that Miss Kotter had located through the Internet.

Sara was having such a good time singing she forgot to look at the clock. "Oops," she cried. "I forgot to feed Stormy. I'd better run home and do it. I'll be right back."

But she didn't come back right away. Not even in 10 minutes. Or 15.

Instead, Sara was running all over her house

looking for her cat. "Stormy!" she called. "Stormy! Where in the world are you?"

Setting aside his chemistry book, Tony joined in the hunt. So did Tank, who ran madly up and down the stairs. But Stormy was nowhere to be found.

"Oh, I wish Mom and Dad were here to help us instead of teaching at the college tonight," Sara moaned. "That poor baby could be outside up in a tree or on the roof or in the street hit by a car or..."

"Let's get help to look for him!" her big brother decided. "You run and tell the Pearsons and the Thomases. I'll get on the phone to call some of the guys I know."

"But shouldn't we call the police or fire department or something?"

"Sara, we don't even know where Stormy is. How could they help us? I think they have more important things to do than search for a missing cat!"

As soon as they heard, the music stopped at the Thomas home. Everyone grabbed a jacket and rushed out into the dark, even Granny B. in her wheelchair. Mr. Moreno's garage door popped open as he ran out, too. So did Sam, with Sonya right behind. Everyone who'd managed to grab a flashlight beamed it under parked cars and up into the neighborhood trees, which were full of new spring leaves.

"This reminds me of the flood night," Sam remarked to Sara and Tony. "Remember — shining the flashlight up through the oak tree?"

But they were both too busy calling, "Here, kitty, kitty, kitty," to hear her.

Up the street they went, then down the street. They looked in front yards, back yards and side yards. They found a couple of stray cats, lots of excited dogs and a highly indignant opossum. But no Stormy.

Finally, Mr. and Mrs. Fields came home. They helped search, too, but they still didn't find Stormy. Her mother gave Sara a hug. "It's very late, sweetie. We'll look again in the morning when it's light. You need to get to bed. It's going to be a warm enough night tonight that Stormy will be okay outside. We'll probably wake up in the morning and he'll be meowing at the back door!"

Sadly, Sara dragged up the stairs to her room. She sat on the edge of her bed, staring into space. She'd never felt so sad in her whole life. Was Stormy gone forever?

Suddenly she heard faint scratching. Then some very plaintive meows from somewhere in her chest of drawers!

She jumped up and started pulling all the drawers open. Out tumbled socks and pajamas and sweaters and underwear all over the floor. Plus one very hungry little kitten!

Even though her friends failed to find him for her, Sara was very glad they all cared enough to try. The next morning, she decided, she'd make sure he was right where he belonged before she left for school. And she made sure to close all of her drawers!

· Good News · from God's Word

Sara's friends all pitched in to help when she needed it. Here is a Bible story about some young women who found they couldn't all help each other all the time.

Ten Young Women Not Working Together

FROM MATTHEW 25:1-13

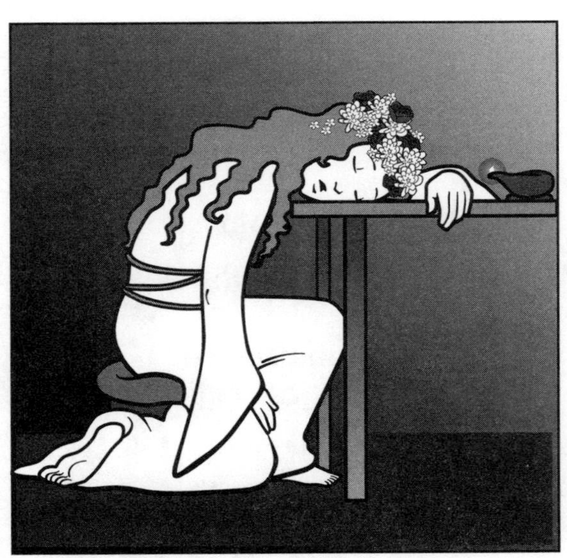

In Bible times, people got married in their homes, not in churches. When a couple decided they liked each other enough to get married, they talked to their families about it. Then they signed an official ketubbah, or marriage contract, in the presence of witnesses. That meant they were officially engaged!

Next came planning for the big wedding feast, usually held at the groom's home. It could last for days! Often, weddings were just for family and immediate friends. But sometimes the entire village was invited.

The day of the wedding, the bridesmaids dressed in their finest and helped the bride into her beautiful wedding gown. But they never knew ahead of time when things would be ready at the other end. After all, this was a huge feast! It might take hours for the food to be ready, for the groom and his friends to finish with their work and for all the other guests to arrive.

When the feast was finally ready, the groom and his attendants went to the bride's home to escort her, her bridesmaids and her family to the big event.

Jesus told about one such Bible-time wedding. The bride had chosen 10 of her friends to be her bridesmaids — an honor and responsibility then, just as it is today. After they and the bride were dressed and ready, it was the custom for them to listen for the first sign of the groom's coming. Then they would rush out to meet him and escort him back to the bride's house.

That was easy to do in the daytime, but harder at night. They didn't have street lights back then, and no flashlights. No street signs and no house numbers! How would the groom find the right house in the dark?

So the bridesmaids all lit oil lamps and had them ready to take when they heard the groom's group approaching. That way there would be plenty of light.

But this groom's party didn't get to the bride's house right away. The bridesmaids waited and waited and waited. Finally it was so late that they just dozed off and fell asleep.

At midnight, they suddenly heard, "Here comes the bridegroom!"

The girls all jumped up. But they had waited so long that the oil in their lamps was just about gone! The lights were sputtering out.

"Oh, my!" one of the girls cried. "I forgot to bring any extra oil! Does someone have some I can borrow?"

Five of the girls had remembered to bring extra oil, just as they were supposed to.

The five who forgot asked, "Please share your oil with us."

"I'm sorry, but we can't!" they replied. "If we did, we'd all run out before we reached the end of our street. Then all of us would be in the dark, including the bridegroom!"

A Verse to Remember

Do two walk together unless they have agreed to do so?

— Amos 3:3

What About You?

Jesus told the story about the bridesmaids to show that we should all help each other to be good Christians. However, each of us is responsible to do everything we can for ourselves, including getting to know and love Jesus as much as possible. How do you grow closer to Jesus? Write three ways below. Not feeling close to Jesus? Try prayer, reading your Bible and maintaining faithful attendance at church. Before you know it, Jesus will be your best friend! He wants to be!

1. ________________________________

2. ________________________________

3. ________________________________

Tell a "Yarn"

Kittens like Stormy love to play with yarn balls. You will, too, after you learn this game.

What You Need

- ball or skein of yarn

What to Do

1. Get your Ponytail Girls or other players together in a circle, seated in chairs or on the floor.

continued on next page...

2. With the yarn in hand, you or someone else starts a story. It can be a familiar fairytale or one you make up as you go along. Be as creative as possible. It can be scary or silly!
3. Tell two or three sentences of your story, then toss the yarn to someone else as you hold the end. She pulls out some yarn and holds on to it as she continues the story for a sentence or two. Then she throws the yarn to still another player.
4. Keep going until everyone has had at least two turns (for a large group) or five turns for a small one. The yarn will twist and turn across your circle!
5. Who wins? Everyone! But you can vote on which player was the most creative.

Joyful Easter Puzzle

Add the Secret Letter "U" for "united" to space 17 of the puzzle on page 26.

Chapter 16

Party Time!

"We won! We won!" Ricardo and Juan cheered as they danced all around the yard. Hearing them, Sneezit and Tank barked wildly.

Maria and Le had just come back from the state science fair. They were exhausted, but grinning from ear to ear.

"Well, not first place," Le explained to the exuberant PTs who had gathered at Maria's to welcome home her and Le. "But we did win third prize in our class. As far as I'm concerned, that's almost as good!"

"We've got to celebrate!" Sam cried. "Let's have a party!"

Then she remembered. "Oh, wait a minute. We're supposed to help sponsor a party for Ma Jones' cousins!"

"Oh, yeah. Plus we promised to have a Mother's Day party for the Whispering Pines folks. Don't forget about that," Jenna added.

"It's almost May Day, too," LaToya said. "That's a fun day to celebrate with baskets of flowers and everything."

Brittany stared at her. " 'May day'? That's what people say when they have an emergency."

Le frowned. "I thought May Day was for the Communists."

"Oh, don't forget Cinco de Mayo," added Maria. "That's a Mexican-American celebration on May fifth."

The girls looked at each other and giggled.

"This is all too much," Sara decided. "There's not enough time for more than one party. Or maybe two. We've got to finish up our family tree project for Mr. Talley, remember?"

Le sighed. "I'm dead tired from going to Riverton. I just want to go home and crash. Can we talk about this tomorrow?"

They could and they did. For final plans, they decided on two parties: one for their own mothers, and one for all the mothers and other women at Whispering Pines, including Ma Jones and her cousins (who were staying at Miss Kotter's). Granny B., Mrs. Greenleaf and her roommate Mrs. Ryan would be invited along to that party, too.

The party at Whispering Pines came first. When the rest of the PTs' Zone 56 group heard about it, they decided to join in again as they had last fall. There was music, refreshments and games. They also got to know Opal and Shirley, the visiting cousins.

Ma Jones was excited for her cousins to be there. "Opal and I went to first grade together. Shirley was already in second," she explained. "Then their family moved to California. We haven't seen each other since. But they haven't changed a bit."

Opal giggled. "Agnes! You know that's not true!"

Ma Jones laughed out loud. "Well, maybe it is an exaggeration. Just a tiny, tiny bit."

Helping the elderly residents have a good time took a lot of effort. Wheelchairs needed to be pushed, the residents' unsteady hands dropped things and some needed help in eating their ice cream and cookies. But seeing the love and joy in their eyes was worth it.

"I sure learned a lot from being with all those grandmothers," Sam admitted to Sonya the next day.

"Me, too. You know, watching them deal with their disabilities made me ashamed to complain about mine. Besides, they gave me some new ideas for the design contest."

"Oh, no, Sonya! There's no time. Remember, everything has to be postmarked by tomorrow night to count!"

"That's okay. I can finish up this evening. Then we can mail our entries tomorrow."

"I have something to mail, too," Maria said. "A beautiful scarf for my Grandmama Gonzalez for Mother's Day. I hope she likes it. I'm so glad she was able to visit us. Mama says we can go visit her down in Texas this summer. Won't that be neat? She's done so much for our family over the years. When the twins were born, Mama was very sick. So Grandmama came and stayed with us. She was just like a second mom to me. Still is. She was so excited to hear I won at the state science fair!"

That day the girls heard some very good news: Ric's uncle was home from the hospital! He still had a lot of physical therapy to undergo. "But he's real upbeat," Ric reported. "Oh, man, is this great or what? Sara's parents are really nice, but I'm ready to go home and help Uncle Max. He's looking forward to it, too. You know, before we just lived together. Now we're family."

But when Maria got home that day, the news that awaited her wasn't as joyous. In fact, it was heartbreaking. "Oh, Maria!" sobbed Lolita. "It's about Grandmama."

"What about her?" Maria said with alarm.

"She's…she's…she's dead!"

· Good News · from God's Word

Maria and her grandmother were very close. Here's a Bible story about another girl and an older woman who loved her.

Nurse Deborah's Loving Service

FROM GENESIS 24:59; 35:8

Rebekah had parents and she had a brother, Laban. But she also had someone else she loved dearly: her nanny, also called a "nurse." We don't know why she had a nanny. Maybe Rebekah's mother was weak when the little girl was born and she needed help.

Deborah fell in love with the baby girl, and Rebekah loved Deborah, too. Deborah soon became a part of the family.

This Deborah isn't the one who was the famous prophetess and musician — the one who led a whole army to victory. We don't know where this Deborah came from or who her family was. Or what kind of training or talents she had.

But we do know she was loving and faithful. In fact, she didn't just help Rebekah's family when she was a little girl. She was still there when Rebekah grew up and married. She even went far away with her to her new home. That's how loyal she was!

Deborah was still working for Rebekah when Rebekah had children of her own: twin boys, Jacob and Esau. What good advice she must have been able to give the new mother. And with two babies, her extra set of loving arms was probably appreciated.

Apparently she was still with the family when those boys grew up and married and had families of their own, and even when Rebekah's grandchildren grew up. But by then she was frail and elderly. Maybe Rebekah took care of her as she got older.

The Bible tells us when Deborah died. We don't know how old she was then, but she was so beloved by everyone that she was buried with honor beneath a huge, beautiful oak tree — like a member of the family.

A Verse to Remember

Follow the way of love.

— 1 Corinthians 14:1

Letters of Love

Do you know what older adults appreciate more than anything? Letters, cards and phone calls from girls like you! Don't send a note just when they give you something (although that's nice, too!), but let them know about your school, sports, hobbies or friends. They might also want to know about your problems so they can pray for you. For easy future reference, write below the names, addresses and phone numbers of your grandparents or others you love.

Name: ____

Address: ______________________________________

Phone: _________________________

Name: ____

Address: ______________________________________

Phone: _________________________

A World of Love

Copy the card pattern at right. Fold it on the dashed lines and color it using crayons, colored pencils or fine-tipped markers. Sign and send your card to one of the people you've listed above.

Joyful Easter Puzzle

Add the Secret Letter "L" for "loving others" to space 14 of the puzzle on page 26.

The World
is Big

Follow the way of love.
1 Corinthians 14:1

**I wish you
were right
here by
my side!**

I Love You!

____

Chapter 17

Trail of Tears

This should have been the best time in Maria's life.

Instead, she was sure it was her worst.

Yes, she and Le sat right up on stage with Principal Anderson and Mrs. Eldridge for school assembly. Everyone clapped and cheered when the announcement was made about their big win at the statewide science fair. They held up their ribbon and prize certificate for everyone to see.

The student council presented each of them with silly stuffed insects and bouquets of lilacs. They smelled wonderful!

And, yes, she was glad to see Sara and Brittany and the other cheerleaders up on stage, too, along with the Madison boys' baseball and girls' softball teams. They led everyone in the new cheer they'd been practicing for upcoming games with Midland.

"Who's up on top?" the cheerleaders shouted.

"Madison, Madison!" the other students shouted back.

"Who's cream of the crop?"

"Madison, Madison!"

"Who can't Midland stop?"

"Madison, Madison, MADISON!"

Usually, Maria would have yelled loudest of all. But not today. Not after her beloved Grandmama had had a stroke and died.

That very evening her whole family was to leave for Texas, just as they had planned earlier. But instead, the trip would be for a funeral, not a happy family vacation. This time Grandmama Gonzalez wouldn't hug and kiss everyone and fill their plates high with delicious food. And she would never do it again.

Of course, Maria knew that her grandmother was in heaven with Jesus. But it hurt just the same. Even when Mr. Talley told Maria she could wait to finish her family project until she got back, it didn't help much.

She was just reminded once more of her loss.

Sam felt awful for Maria, and almost guilty. After all, her own grandmothers were still alive and well. So was LaToya's Granny B.

"I know," Le sighed when Sam talked with her later. "I never even knew either of my grandmothers. They were killed in the war before I was born. But I love them just the same. My father's mother was a Christian, so I know for sure I'll see her one day. It's wonderful to know she's with Jesus. But I wish I had a grandmother right here to hug and talk to."

When Maria's family finally got the car packed for the long drive to Texas, all the PTs were there to see them off, tears and all. "*Adios!*" they called. "Hurry back!"

Sam just couldn't get over feeling sad about it all — not when she and Sonya mailed off their contest entries, and not even when she got back to her family tree project. Everything seemed so sad!

For instance, why did her Grandma Pearson have to give up her career in fashion design to move back to Michigan? Why didn't Grandpa Pearson move to New York to be with her?

In her family tree, Sam found out about some relatives who had starved to death in the Irish famine of the 1800's. That wasn't fair! Why did it happen?

Sam wasn't the only sad one. Sonya felt terrible as she read about the Trail of Tears in 1838, when her Cherokee ancestors were forced to leave their homes and march across the U.S. in freezing weather. Thousands died. Many of the Cherokees were Christian believers. They hadn't done anything wrong. Why did God allow it? And what about the accident that killed her mother and injured Sonya? Couldn't God have prevented it if He wanted to?

LaToya was just as discouraged when she learned about all her relatives who had been captured in Africa and brought to America as slaves. Some were tortured and killed. Where was God when that happened?

Jenna found out one of her relatives had been a missionary in India. This cousin had helped many orphans there, but then she ended up dying of malaria.

So the PTs were all feeling discouraged that Thursday evening when they met to plan Saturday's party for their mothers. Miss Kotter was there, too. She had just finished seeing off Ma Jones' visiting cousins at the train station.

They had a lot of planning to do, of course. They decided to make it a lunch party on Saturday afternoon at the Pearsons' and call it a "Mommy 'N Me Tea." Then they needed to figure out what kind of food they would have, how they would babysit the kids while their moms got together, how everyone would get there and so on.

But Sam couldn't get her worries out of her mind. "Miss Kotter," she finally asked, "why does God let bad things happen?"

"People have been asking that for a long time, Sam," her teacher replied. "I certainly asked it when my parents died. I asked it when Bob and I broke up last winter. But I do know this: God is still in charge. And He can be trusted to do what is right for us.

"That was the lesson in the book of Job. Remember, terrible things happened to him. His friends said it was all his fault. Well, sometimes bad things are our own fault. For instance, if we run out in front of traffic on the freeway, we're asking for trouble. If we eat too much candy, we'll get cavities in our teeth. If we refuse to study, we'll flunk that class.

"But other times only God has the answers. And the one thing I do know is that God's answers are the right answers. Because He knows everything, including what's best for me. And for all of you!"

· Good News · from God's Word

Even though many bad things that happen to us aren't our faults, some are. That's what Miriam learned one day.

Miriam's Need to Change

from Numbers 12:1-15

Remember Miriam? She was Moses' and Aaron's big sister. She's the one who watched over Moses while he floated in a basket in the Nile River. She was also the one who talked to the princess and suggested her own mother as the babysitter for her baby brother.

Miriam was smart and she loved God. She

became well-known as a musician and a prophetess (someone who tells people about God's Word). Then when Miriam was quite elderly, probably in her 80s or even 90s, Moses led the people out of Egypt and across the Red Sea. After they were all across safely, she led the women in a celebration. Miriam sang and played the tambourine. She was probably very proud of her brother.

When the Israelites reached Mt. Sinai, God gave His law to His people. We know that law as the Ten Commandments. He also said that Aaron and his sons would be His priests.

Then something happened. Did you ever get jealous of your brothers or sisters? Or get into arguments with them? That's what happened to Miriam.

"Moses has gotten big-headed," she complained to Aaron. "But he has no right to. I'm his big sister. Besides, he didn't marry an Israelite. He married someone he met out in the desert." In Bible times, marrying outside of one's culture was viewed unfavorably.

"You're right," Aaron agreed. "I'm his big brother. Besides, he acts like God only talks to him. God talks to you and me, too. I'm the high priest! You're a prophetess! We're just as important as he is!" And they both told Moses so.

Moses didn't know what to do. But God did.

"I want all three of you to come to the tabernacle!" God said. "At once!"

There God made His presence known in a great cloud. "Miriam, Aaron," he said. "I want to tell you something. Yes, I speak to you. But not in the very special way I reveal My truth to your brother Moses. He is a very special servant for me. Why did you dare to talk to him that way?"

Because Miriam was most at fault, God covered her with leprosy, a dreaded skin disease. Today, leprosy is called Hansen's disease and it is curable. But in Bible times there was no cure.

Both her brothers were horrified for Miriam. Aaron told Moses he was sorry for what he said. Moses begged God to heal their sister.

"I will heal her in a week," God replied. "Until then, she will stay sick."

Miriam was sick for the whole week. God gave her a week to think about what she did wrong and to ask God to forgive her. She also needed to ask Moses to forgive her. Miriam used her week in sickness to change her attitude and to decide to do better in the future.

A Verse to Remember

"I know the plans I have for you," declares the Lord "...plans to give you hope and a future."

— Jeremiah 29:11

What About You?

Can you remember losing a loved one to illness or an accident? If so, write that person's name here: ______________________________

How did you feel about it at the time?

____

____

How do you feel about it now?

____

____

If you still have pain inside when you think about it, ask God to help you. He can. He is the "God of all comfort" (2 Corinthians 1:3).

Joyful Easter Puzzle

Add the Secret Letter "S" for "sure of God's love" to space 3 of the puzzle on page 26.

Chapter 18

I Kid You Not!

"Well, that's that!" Sam announced as she turned in her social studies project. She had included all her work in a special notebook along with plenty of pictures and a taped interview with her Grandma Pearson.

Everyone else in the class had huge projects, too. All, that is, except Ric.

"We don't know where my parents are," he explained to Mr. Talley. "So I couldn't ask them anything.

And Uncle Max didn't know much himself. Besides, he's been in the hospital. But I did find out that one of my ancestors was a Spanish pirate."

Grinning, he added, "I figure he's the one I took after. Anyway, I wrote about him."

"Wow! A pirate!" Kevin exclaimed. "What was his name?"

"Enrico Moreno. Just like Maria's last name."

"Wow!" Josh replied. "Wonder if you're related?"

"Sure," Jenna quipped. "We're all related, if you go back to Adam and Eve!"

Then their teacher let everyone tell what the project had meant to them. Some had been fascinated by what they discovered. "I figured my parents are farmers and their parents were farmers, and it would all be so bo-o-ring," Garrett confessed. "Then I discovered that some had been Amish farmers. Some were farmers who had to run away from persecution in Russia. Some were scientists who developed special hybrids of corn. And then suddenly they weren't so boring anymore."

"Speaking of persecution," Allison said, "I found out that some of my relatives died in the Holocaust in Germany. Some of my other relatives were soldiers who helped free the survivors from those concentration camps. I cried when I read all that!"

Sara giggled. "Talking about bawling, look what I taped on the front of my report." It was a picture of her as a tiny baby, red hair and all —

bawling like crazy!

After school, Sam remarked, "Putting your baby picture on your report was a great idea, Sara."

"Yeah," LaToya added. "It reminded me about tomorrow and the kids we'll be babysitting then. Any more stuff we need to do for our 'Mommy 'n Me Tea'?"

Le checked her list. "Well, I took Maria's family off the list, since they won't be here. So here's what we need to get ready for the mothers: card tables, tablecloths, sandwiches, teabags, teacups, saucers and plates, cookies, napkins, teapots, aprons and silverware. Anything else?"

Mommy N Me Tea

- ✓ Card tables
- ✓ tablecloths
- ✓ sandwiches
- ✓ tea bags
- ✓ teacups
- ✓ saucers
- ✓ plates
- ✓ cookies

"Don't forget folding chairs," Sonya reminded her. "And a place to hang up coats and umbrellas if it's raining. And flowers on the tables."

"What do we need to have for the kids?"

"Peanut butter, jelly, bread, milk, fruit punch, paper cups and plates. And lots of toys, games and videos."

"A place for the twins to sleep, too," Jenna reminded them. "And to change their diapers and warm their bottles."

It all sounded so exciting. Sam could hardly sleep that night. The next morning she gulped down her breakfast so she could vacuum the living room and clean up the kitchen. Then when she heard the weather report, she could hardly contain her glee: fair and warmer, with highs in the upper 70s. And no wind! That meant they could set up the mothers' tables on the deck, where they could enjoy the gorgeous spring flowers, bushes and trees.

Soon the PTs came over to join her. All except Maria, of course. By the time the mothers and children arrived, everything was ready. Le helped all the women find a place at the tables. LaToya directed the children down to the basement rec room. Sara and Brittany helped serve. Le serenaded everyone with her violin.

"This is just marvelous, girls," Mrs. Boorsma cried. "What a great opportunity for us moms to get to know each other better."

Granny B. stayed in the kitchen, taking care of the food. LaToya and Sam entertained the older children downstairs. Sonya and Jenna took care of the youngest ones in Petie's room.

"Isn't it great that we're all so organized?" Sam remarked happily.

Of course, that was before baby Noel got sick and threw up all over everything. And before Petie and Michael and Nicholas got into a fight over whose turn it was to play with the toy train. And before Suzie and Lolita decided to play "beauty shop" with scissors from the crayon box. And before Katie fell down the stairs. And before baby Holly started crying and wouldn't stop.

"Kids! Aaargh!" Sam stormed to herself. "I can't wait until this day is over."

But…

That was before Suzie threw her arms around Sam and whispered, "I just love you! You're my favoritest person." And before Petie kissed Katie's "boo-boo" so "it'll be all better." And before all the children decided to play "big church" and asked Jenna to read them a Bible story and help them pray. Sam changed her mind. Kids were pretty wonderful, after all!

· Good News · from God's Word

Children are precious gifts from God. That's why your parents love you so much, and why you should treasure your brothers, sisters and all young children. This Bible story tells about some brave women who realized God's love for babies and little children, so they did something about it. Even though their own lives were in danger!

Shiphrah and Puah's Brave Decision

FROM EXODUS 1:6-22

In Bible times, when babies were born their mothers had no hospitals to go to. There weren't any hospitals! Instead, babies were born at home.

There weren't many doctors then, either. The doctors that existed were busy helping kings and queens and "important" people. Not poor ones. And certainly not slaves.

When God's people were slaves in Egypt, instead of doctors they used specially-trained women called midwives to help them have babies. Today, some women still use midwives if they want to have their babies at home. But these certified midwives now work under the guidance of doctors.

There were only two midwives for all of the Israelites because the Pharaoh, their slave master, didn't want to give up any women slaves to midwifery. He wanted the rest of his slaves to work in the fields, building temples and palaces. The names of the two midwives were Shiphrah and Puah. One day, Shiphrah and Puah were called to the Pharaoh's palace. It was scary for slaves to be called by the Pharaoh. He was so powerful, he could have them killed in an instant!

But into the grand palace they went. "All right, you two," he commanded. "I know you're midwives. Well, from now on there are going to be some changes. You can go ahead and let all the baby girls live. But you're to kill all the baby boys the minute they are born. Understand?"

Oh, they understood all right. This wicked ruler wanted them to commit murder. Not just once, but over and over again. The knew that God did not approve of murder. Because they loved God, they wanted to obey him. So they disobeyed the Pharaoh.

He called them in again. "Why didn't you kill all those baby boys?" he roared.

They simply pretended that they hadn't been around when the baby boys were born. After all, there were a lot of pregnant women for just two midwives to handle. They couldn't get to them all! But it wasn't true. The midwives were just determined not to sin against God. Besides, God wasn't the only one who loved little babies: so did the mothers and their families. And so did Shiphrah and Puah!

God was so pleased with the two midwives' bravery, he helped them fall in love and marry and have children of their own.

A Verse to Remember

This is what Jesus said about little children:

Whoever welcomes one of these little children in my name welcomes me.

— ***Mark 9:37***

Bible-time Babysitters

Here's a fun Bible quiz. Match each caregiver on the left with the baby she cared for on the right. The answers are on page 189.

1. Elizabeth
2. Naomi
3. Miriam
4. Hannah
5. Eve
6. Mary, Joseph's wife
7. Sarah
8. Jehosheba
9. Deborah, the nurse
10. Rebekah

A. Isaac
B. Abel
C. Joash
D. Rebekah
E. Obed
F. Esau and Jacob
G. John the Baptist
H. Moses
I. Jesus
J. Samuel

Joyful Easter Puzzle

Add the Secret Letter "J" for "just crazy about kids" to space 18 of the puzzle on page 26.

Chapter 19

Branching Out

Sam flicked a blossom petal off her nose and found a more comfortable position on her beach towel. No, not on the beach — out in her backyard, taking a Saturday afternoon break with two of the PTs.

It was a lovely May day. The grass was as soft and green as a plush carpet. Overhead, sunlight filtered through the blossoms and leaves of Petie's favorite plant: an old apple tree in full bloom.

Sam remembered that her dad had said that

apple tree was one of the main reasons he and her mom bought that house. It had been planted long ago, when that part of Circleville was still farmland. Now the nearest farm was five miles away. But the apple tree was still there.

When Sam was younger, she and her dad built a tree house with a rope ladder in the tree's sturdy branches. Now Petie and his pals claimed it.

Sam pointed to a fluffy cloud drifting overhead. "Look! I can't decide if that's an elephant or a camel."

Le moved over on her beach towel and squinted. "I vote for a dragon. No, look, it's already changed. Now I say it looks more like…"

"A dull, ordinary cloud," Sara finished for her, giggling. "Sam, can you remember us playing this same game when we were little? And now we're practically teenagers. I can remember when Tony had to lift me up to get me into your tree house. Now my head touches the bottom of it. All of a sudden, it seems like I'm a different me. I can't even wear the same shoes I bought last fall. It's like I've outgrown myself and now I'm wearing someone else's body."

As the other two thought about that, Stormy jumped all over them, trying to catch the blossom petals before they fell. Then he discovered a bright yellow butterfly and zoomed around madly chasing it.

"Even little Stormy's growing up," Le observed. "Remember when you two found him up that tree during the flood? He was so tiny he could fit into Tony's pocket. Now he thinks he owns the world."

Just then, Petie ran into the back yard, with Juan and Ricardo in hot pursuit. "Up to the spaceship, men!" Petie cried. "Defend it from the aliens!"

All three scrambled up the tree trunk and into their hideaway.

Le grinned. "Oh, great. Now we're aliens!" Then a few moments later she said, "I'm glad the Morenos are back from their trip. Wonder where Maria is?"

"Probably helping her mom catch up with laundry and stuff," Sara answered. "At least their yard and garden are okay. Tony went over after school every day and watered for them. You know, I have to say he is a pretty cool guy, even if he's a pain sometimes!"

"Moms can be pains, too," Sam griped. "I had so much I wanted to do this morning — starting with sleeping in! But, no. Mom said, 'Your room is a mess. Your closet's a mess. Your floor's a mess.' I felt like saying, 'Well, my hair's a mess, too. So's my face. And so are my grades. And so's my life.' I didn't, but I really felt like it.

"But then when I went through my closet this morning I noticed that I had a lot of stuff that didn't even fit me any more. So I asked Mom, and she let me throw it all into a big bag for the rescue mission. It was a real quick way to clean up my closet! But now I don't have anything to wear. I don't know if growing up is a thrill or just a drag. It sure complicates things. I kinda liked being just a kid."

Sara chewed on a sweet clover blossom. "Well, being a kid was fun. But Tony says being a teenager is, too. Remember when we talked about what we want to do when we grow up? I wanted to be a movie star or an astronaut or a dentist. Now I'm thinking about getting serious with my ice skating at the rink this summer. What about you two? What do you think will happen with you?"

Le twirled around a long blade of grass as Stormy chased it. "I think I'll do concerts like my mom. And travel a lot. What about you, Sam?"

"Well, Grandma Pearson got me all excited about fashion design. I probably won't win that contest. But I'm going to take a sewing class this summer. That will help me understand how clothes are put together. And besides, I've got all that empty room in my closet to fill up! Oh, and I'll be babysitting Petie and Suzie part-time, and helping Petie get to softball practice."

Brittany suddenly came running into the back yard. Startled, Stormy scrambled up the tree and into the tree house. Shrieks exploded. "Invading space alien!" Juan shouted. And the three boys jumped down and ran away.

Brittany giggled. "Oh, girls! I just had to tell you something that's absolutely cool! You know how my parents have been going to counseling. Well, guess what? They've decided they really love each other, after all. Next month they're going to a special weekend retreat for couples — a Christian one! I am so happy!"

Just then, Maria's and Jenna's heads popped over the fence from Maria's yard. Maria held up a racket. "Tennis, anyone?" she said with a grin.

Sam stared at her. "Hey, since when did you play tennis?"

"Since my trip. Besides the funeral, I spent a lot of time there with my cousin Rosalita. She's on the tennis team at her college. She showed me how to play and she says I'm a natural. We're on our way to the tennis courts down at the park. Anyone want to come along?"

"I found an old racket of Dad's to use," Jenna explained. "A can of balls, too. I've been around babies all morning and I'm dying to do something more grown-up."

Sonya wheeled into the yard with LaToya. "Hey, what is this, some kind of meeting? Listen, everyone, LaToya and I have great news!"

LaToya went first. "Tina's graduating next week and she has a job already at the Midland Hospital. I'm going to work with Miss Kotter at Whispering Pines and the rescue mission this summer."

Sonya nodded. "Me, too. Plus something else really great. You know about wheelchair basketball? Well, there's a big tournament in July in Summer City. Tony and Miss Kotter are going to help me train.

"But for the biggest news of all…drum roll, please! Miss Kotter's going to a Christian concert tonight with Pastor Andy. And tomorrow after church she's going out to dinner with Dad and me!"

Miss Kotter was dating Pastor Andy? The PTs looked at each other and grinned. Wow! Life sure could be great, after all!

· Good News · from God's Word

Here's someone from the Bible who discovered how wonderful life could be.

Mary Rejoices in the Lord

FROM ACTS 12:12-17

"Mary" was a very popular name in New Testament times. That was Jesus' mother's name, of course. Then there was Mary Magdalene; Martha's sister, Mary; and James and John's mother, Mary. It was also the name of another woman, the mother of a young

Christian named John Mark. Since most people didn't have last names then, having so many friends with the same first name must have been very confusing!

This particular Mary was wealthy and lived in Jerusalem. Apparently she was a widow, which was sad. But something wonderful and new filled her life to replace that sadness. She heard about Jesus and became a Christian!

Mary was so happy about knowing Jesus that she opened her large home to other Christians. Worship services and Bible studies were held there, as well as prayer times. The Christians rushed to her home to pray for Peter when he was in prison. Of course, they were terrified that Peter would be killed. When God set him free, Mary and the other Christians were thrilled!

Mary's love for the Lord spilled over to her servants. We know that at least one, a young woman named Rhoda, loved the Lord, too. Maybe it was Mary who helped her know about Jesus.

Mary had something else to rejoice about. Her own son, John Mark, was a believer, too. He was a young man, but he was a shining light for Jesus. Her nephew Barnabas was also a Christian. Barnabas' hometown was Cyprus, an island in the Mediterranean Sea over 200 miles away (Acts 4:36). So Barnabas often traveled to Jerusalem and stayed with his Aunt Mary (Colossians 4:10). John Mark and Barnabas became missionaries for Jesus. Later, Mary's son wrote one of the four Gospels in the New Testament, the book we call "Mark."

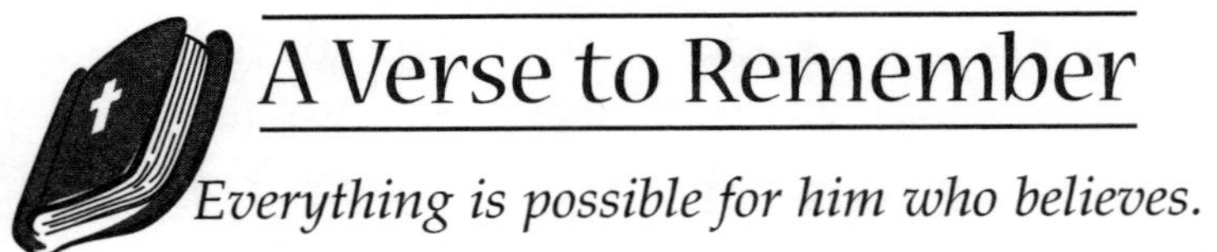

A Verse to Remember

Everything is possible for him who believes.

— Mark 9:23

What About You?

Do you sometimes get scared when you think about the future? Do you feel unattractive, klutzy, lonely, unloved, inadequate or ridiculed? If so, write here what is troubling you.

____

____

____

There is great news for you! God doesn't see you as a failure, a loser, unattractive or untalented. He doesn't just think you're the greatest. He knows you are! He has special plans for you. He wants you to believe in Him and in yourself. Don't worry if you suddenly don't feel like yourself, as Sam described. Your body is changing. You are growing from the wonderful girl you are now into the even more wonderful woman God plans for you to be. You're God's beloved daughter. His royal princess!

Joyful Easter Puzzle

Add the Secret Letter "S" for "seeing life's possibilities" to space 5 of the puzzle on page 26. Fill in the joyful message. Share it with someone!

The Ponytail Girls Club

Would you like to be a part of a Ponytail Girls Club? You can be a PT yourself, of course. But it's much more fun if one of your friends joins with you. Or even five or six of them! There is no cost. You can read the Ponytail Girls stories together, do the puzzles and other activities, study the Bible stories, and learn the Bible verses.

If your friends buy their own Ponytail Girls books, you can all write in yours at the same time. Arrange a regular meeting time and place, and plan to do special things together, just like the PTs do in the stories, such as shopping, Bible study, homework, or helping others.

Trace or copy the membership cards on page 183 and give one to each PT in your group.

Membership Cards

Trace or photocopy these cards. Fill them out, date them, and give one to each member of your Ponytail Girls Club. Be sure to put your membership card in your wallet or another special place for safekeeping!

____

is a member in good standing of
The Ponytail Girls Club.

____
Signature

____
Date

____

is a member in good standing of
The Ponytail Girls Club.

____
Signature

____
Date

Bible Verses to Remember and Share

These are the Bible verses the Ponytail Girls studied throughout this book. Write them on pretty paper and learn them. Share your favorite with someone else!

The eternal God is your refuge.
~ Deuteronomy 33:27

The people worked with all their heart.
~ Nehemiah 4:6

Show me your ways, O Lord, teach me your paths.
~ Psalm 25:4

Sing to the Lord with thanksgiving.
~ Psalm 147:7

She…works with eager hands.
~ Proverbs 31:13

"I know the plans I have for you," declares the Lord…"plans to give you hope and a future."
~ Jeremiah 29:11

Do two walk together unless they have agreed to do so?
~ Amos 3:3

Let your light shine before men.
~ Matthew 5:16

continued on next page…

*Whoever does the will of my father in heaven
is my brother and sister.*
~ Matthew 12:50

Everything is possible for him who believes.
~ Mark 9:23

*Whoever welcomes one of these little children
in my name welcomes me.*
~ Mark 9:37

*They took palm branches and went out to meet Him,
shouting, "Hosanna! Blessed is he who comes
in the name of the Lord!"*
~ John 12:13

Follow the way of love.
~ 1 Corinthians 14:1

God...raised Christ from the dead.
~ 1 Corinthians 15:15

Godly sorrow brings repentance.
~ 2 Corinthians 7:10

Sing and make music in your heart to the Lord.
~ Ephesians 5:19

*Always giving thanks to God the father for
everything, in the name of our Lord Jesus Christ.*
~ Ephesians 5:20

In your anger do not sin.
~ Ephesians 4:26

I thank my God every time I remember you.
~ Philippians 1:3

Glossary (glos/ərē)

Caesarea: *sess-ah-ree-ah*

Capernaum: *kuh-purr-nay-yum*

Cinco de Mayo: *sink-oh day my-oh*

Enrico: *on-ree-koh*

Ephraim: *ee-fray-eem*

Forsythia: *for-sith-ee-uh*

Hola: *hello*

Ketubbah: *keh-too-bah*

Merab: *me-rab*

Michal: *my-kal*

Pharisees: *fair-uh-sees*

Puah: *poo-ah*

Salome: *saw-loh-may*

Sheerah: *she-rah*

Shiphrah: *shi-frah*

Sinai: *sigh-nigh*

Synagogue: *sin-uh-gog*

Answers to Puzzles

Chapter 4

Up a Tree?, pp. 52-53

1. E
2. J
3. F
4. G
5. A
6. C
7. D
8. B
9. I
10. H

Chapter 5

Bible Praise Time, pp. 61-62

1. G
2. J
3. H
4. I
5. C
6. F
7. A
8. E
9. D
10. B

Chapter 7

April Fool's, p. 79

True: 1, 2, 7, 9
Jokes: 3, 4, 5, 6, 8, 10

Chapter 9

You Can Count on It, p. 95

Anything worth doing is worth doing well.

Chapter 10

A Real Cross-Word Puzzle, p. 103

For God so loved the world that he gave his one and only son.

Chapter 12

It's in There Somewhere, pp. 118-119

1. Matthew, Mark, Luke, John
2. Genesis
3. Exodus
4. False
5. False
6. Revelation
7. Rome
8. Numbers
9. Psalms
10. Proverbs
11. Daniel
12. Lamentations
13. Jonah
14. Malachi
15. Moses

Chapter 13
Nursery Nonsense, pp. 127-128
1. H
2. F
3. L
4. I
5. J
6. B
7. K
8. A
9. D
10. E
11. G
12. C

Chapter 14
Gone to Pot, p. 138

Chapter 18
Bible Time Babysitters, p. 172
1. G
2. E
3. H
4. J
5. B
6. I
7. A
8. C
9. D
10. F

Joyful Easter Puzzle

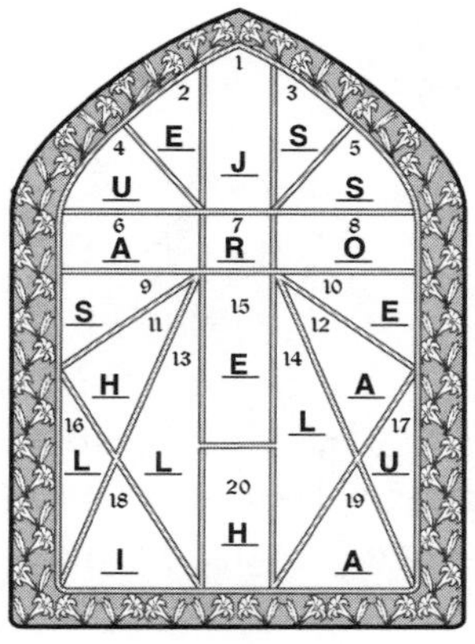

JESUS AROSE!
HALLELUJAH!

Attention: Christian babysitters!

This is the only manual you will need to be the best babysitter on the block— and to share about God with others. *The Official Christian Babysitting Guide* is packed with everything you want to know about taking care of kids. Step-by-step instructions will help you learn the best ways to change a diaper, feed a baby or calm a scared child. Plus, get ideas for keeping kids busy with pages and pages of crafts, games, snacks and songs. Most importantly, you will find Scriptures and strategies for serving God as you serve families. Get *The Official Christian Babysitting Guide* and find out how you can be a blessing as you babysit!

LP 48021
ISBN 1-58411-027-9

You're not just a girl. You're one of God's Girls!

Hey, girls, get ready to add some sparkle to your look and a lot of fun to your life. *God's Girls* is packed with tips and ideas to help you make cool crafts. Plus you will read about Bible women and learn how to be a faithful Christian. There is even space included for you to write your deepest thoughts and dreams. So come on and join the party…you are one of *God's Girls!*

LP48011
ISBN 1-58411-020-1

LP48012
ISBN 1-58411-021-X

GET A FREE SCRUNCHIE!

The Ponytail Girls love to give each other gifts. Here is one for you: a **free** scrunchie! Just fill out the form below and enclose a check or money order for $2.20 to cover shipping and handling. Also, we would love to hear more about you and your thoughts, so please fill out the form on the other side, too.

My name

My address

City State Zip

Parent's signature

My birth date: ____/____/____
month/day/year

❑ Send me a scrunchie and a free catalog!
My check or money order for $2.20 is enclosed.

❑ Send my friend a free catalog, too!

My friend's name

Address

City State Zip

Mail this form to: Ponytails • Legacy Press • P.O. Box 261129 • San Diego, CA 92196

Which of *The Ponytail Girls* books have you read?

- ❑ *Meet the Ponytail Girls*
- ❑ *The Impossible Christmas Present*
- ❑ *Lost on Monster Mountain*
- ❑ *A Stormy Spring*
- ❑ *Escape from Camp Porcupine*

My favorite PT is: ______________________________

I am in a Ponytail Girls Club. ❑ yes ❑ no

I am in another club. ❑ yes ❑ no

The name of my club is: ______________________________

My favorite thing to do is: ______________________________

My favorite book is: ______________________________

because: ______________________________

My favorite magazine is: ______________________________

because: ______________________________